HIGH POINT

SUCCESS IN LANGUAGE • LITERATURE • CONTENT

Practice Book

LEVEL A

HAMPTON-BROWN

Practice Book Contents

UNIT 1 MIND MAP

Identity

DIRECTIONS Use the mind map to show what you are like. Draw pictures or write sentences. Read each selection in this unit. Add to the map ideas you learn about identity.

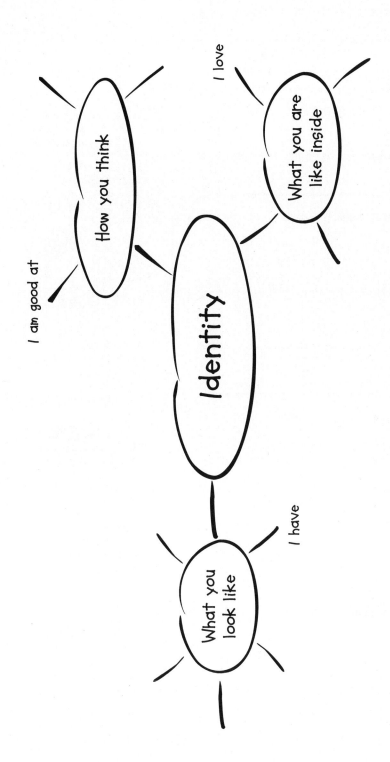

BUILD LANGUAGE AND VOCABULARY

Describe a Friend

DIRECTIONS Write what the people might say. Use present tense verbs and adjectives from the word box.

Verbs	Adjectives			
am	friendly	silly	quiet	clever
is	kind	happy	wise	helpful
are	strong	active	graceful	cute

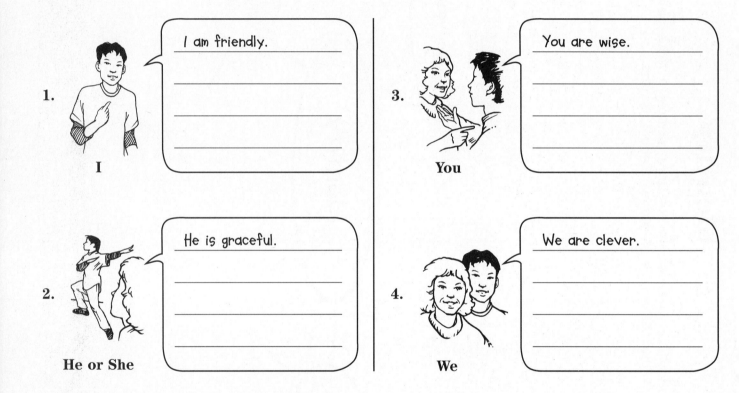

1. I am friendly. _____
   I

2. He is graceful. _____
   He or She

3. You are wise. _____
   You

4. We are clever. _____
   We

DIRECTIONS Now tell about yourself and a friend.

Example:

5. Tell about yourself.   I am clever.

6. Tell about your partner.   She is clever.

7. Trade papers and talk to your partner.   You are clever.

8. Tell about both partners.   We are clever.

Discovery Words

New Words

character

discover

intelligent

irresponsible

irritable

lazy

merits

optimistic

positive

shortcomings

Use New Words in Context

DIRECTIONS Read each sentence. Write the correct word.

1. I am smart. I am _____ intelligent _____ .

2. I am nice to everyone. That is part of my _____ .

3. I have some bad points. They are my _____ .

4. I have some good points. They are my _____ .

5. Sometimes I don't sleep well. Then I feel upset

   and _____ .

6. I want to learn about myself. I want to _____

   what I like to do.

7. I am hopeful. I am _____ .

8. Sometimes I don't want to work. Then I am _____ .

9. Sometimes I do not keep my promises. Then I

   am _____ .

10. I see the best in everything. I am _____ .

Relate Words

DIRECTIONS Work with a group. Write the new words where
they belong in the chart.

Discover Your Character

Merits	Shortcomings
positive	lazy

GRAMMAR: PRESENT TENSE

Just Another Day

walk

ride

wave

dig

drink

play

write

read

see

sing

eat

think

shout

Present Tense

Present tense verbs tell what is happening now, or what happens all the time.

I **walk** to school.
María **rides** her bike.

How to Play
Just Another Day

Play in a group of three. One person is "the judge."

1. Each player chooses a game piece, and uses a coin to move:

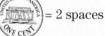 = 1 space

= 2 spaces

2. Look at the picture and read the verb. Use the present tense of the verb to tell what you do. Then tell what someone else does.

Example:
I play the violin.
Yolanda plays the trumpet.

3. Score 1 point for each correct sentence. "The judge" decides.

The person with the most points at the end of the game wins!

4

SUM IT UP

Classify Ideas

DIRECTIONS Read what Irma says about herself. Complete the chart.

Who Is Irma?

I want to discover
new sources of energy.
I want to discover
how to keep the earth clean.
I want to discover myself.

Up to now I know what my merits are.
I am creative.
I am strong.
I am kind.

I know what my shortcomings are.
I am forgetful.
I am shy.

I want to discover more about myself.

Things Irma Knows About Herself	Things Irma Wants to Discover
Irma is _____creative_____ .	Irma wants to discover _____ _____ .
She is _____ .	
She is _____ .	She wants to discover _____
She is _____ .	
She is _____ .	She wants to discover _____ _____ .

DIRECTIONS Write two sentences. Tell what Irma is like.
Tell what she wants to discover.

1. _____

2. _____

Describe People

DIRECTIONS Complete the captions for each picture. Use *is*, *am*, or *are*. Choose words from the box to tell what the people are like.

Character Traits			
wise	brave	helpful	thoughtful
kind	upset	careful	positive
smart	caring	loving	intelligent
afraid	active	alert	responsible

Present Tense

Present tense verbs tell what is happening now or what happens all the time. **Am**, **is**, and **are** are present tense verbs.

Use **am** with the word **I**.
I **am** brave.

Use **is** with the words **he** or **she**.
He **is** optimistic.

Use **are** with the words **we**, **you**, or **they**.
They **are** silly.

True Heroes

1.

Jessica and Pedro ___are alert_____ .

They _____ .

2.

Jessica _____ .

Pedro _____ .

3.

Pedro says, "I _____ ."

He _____ .

4.

The friends _____ .

They _____ .

MORE ABOUT VERBS Now draw your own cartoon. Write a caption for each picture. Use present tense verbs.

RESEARCH SKILLS

Using Alphabetical Order

DIRECTIONS Read the words in the box. Write the words in alphabetical order.

scale	invention	pollution
life	medicine	measure
plant	scientist	nature
name	information	light

Alphabetical Order

Many books list subjects in **alphabetical order**. Each group of words below is in alphabetical order.

electronics	echo	light
farming	egret	lime
medicine	element	liquid

1. _____information_____

2. _____

3. _____

4. _____

5. _____

6. _____

7. _____

8. _____

9. _____

10. _____

11. _____

12. _____

DIRECTIONS Where can you find an article about each subject? Write the number of the volume.

Alphabetical Order in an Encyclopedia

An **encyclopedia** is a set of books. Each book is a **volume**. Each volume has **articles** that give facts about many different subjects. Volumes and subjects are in alphabetical order.

Encyclopedia Volumes

13. leukemia _____

14. peanut _____

15. Carver, George Washington _____

16. Elion, Gertrude _____

17. space _____

18. Curie, Marie _____

© Hampton-Brown

Research a Scientist

DIRECTIONS Follow the steps to research a scientist.

1 **Think about what you will do. Write answers to the questions.**

1. Which scientist will I research? _____

2. What is the best key word to use? _____

3. What other key words might help me find information?

   _____

   _____

4. What do I need to know about the scientist?

   _____

   _____

   _____

   _____

Marie Curie discovered radium. Radium is helpful in the treatment of cancer.

5. What do I already know about the scientist?

   _____

   _____

   _____

6. Where will I look for information? Who can help me find it? _____

   _____

   _____

2 **Choose your sources. Write the titles or names.**

☐ book   ☐ Web site   ☐ teacher   ☐ other

_____   _____   _____   _____

_____   _____   _____   _____

_____   _____   _____   _____

_____   _____   _____   _____

3 Take notes. Learn how on page 369 of your Handbook.

Notecards

Research Question

Source

Notes

What did _____ discover?

—

—

—

George Washington Carver
developed hundreds of
products from peanuts.

Why were _____ 's discoveries important?

—

—

—

4 Make a poster. Look at your notes. Decide what you will show
on your poster.

A Class Full of Questions

DIRECTIONS Work with a partner. Write questions to ask classmates.

Questions

Use a **question** to ask for information.

Who sits next to you?
When do you eat dinner?

Who

Who is your favorite actor?

What

Where

Why

?

When

How

MORE QUESTIONS AND ANSWERS Work with a group.
Take turns asking and answering questions.

Words About Moving

New Words

adapt

culture

enjoy

felt

island

miss

situation

strange

Use New Words in Context

DIRECTIONS Read each sentence. Circle the correct word.
Then write the sentence.

1. I moved here from the ____(island)/ situation____ of Taiwan.

   I moved here from the island of Taiwan.

2. I was sad and began to ____miss / enjoy____ my friends in Taiwan.

   _____

3. Then I started to ____felt / adapt____ to my new life.

   _____

4. Now I know more about the ____culture / strange____ of the U.S.

   _____

Use Context Clues

DIRECTIONS Write about a trip to an island. Use the new words.

5. I went to an ____island____ .

6. The island was _____ at first.

7. I _____ different.

8. I was in a new _____ .

9. Then I began to _____ the interesting art and music there.

10. The people have an interesting

    _____ .

11. I began to _____ to

    this new place.

12. Then I went home. I started to

    _____ the island.

Could I Ask You a Question?
LEVEL A TE page T24

11

Unit 1 | Identity

Welcome to Puerto Rico!

DIRECTIONS Read the passage. Underline all the nouns. Then write the nouns in the chart where they belong.

"Hello and welcome to <u>Puerto Rico</u>! My <u>name</u> is <u>Julio</u>. The driver of our bus is Mili. I am your guide. I hope you like our island. We have beautiful mountains. You can see many rare plants and animals in our forests.

This is San Juan. More than 500,000 people live here. Our city is full of buildings and automobiles. You can see visitors and workers. Our signs are written in Spanish, but many Puerto Ricans also speak English. Our country is a great place to be!"

People	Places	Things and Ideas
Julio	Puerto Rico	name

MORE ABOUT NOUNS Look back at "Could I Ask You a Question?" Add more nouns about Puerto Rico to the chart. Then use your nouns to tell a partner about Puerto Rico.

Make Comparisons

DIRECTIONS Read about Eduardo. Tell how you and Eduardo are alike.
Tell how you and Eduardo are different. Use the chart.

Eduardo lives in Puerto Rico with his family. He has a brother and a sister. He is in the seventh grade. He really likes math and sports. After school he plays soccer.

Eduardo plays soccer.

All About Eduardo	All About Me
Eduardo is in the seventh grade.	

DIRECTIONS Read each question. Write the answers.

How are you and Eduardo the same?

1. We both _____ .

2. We both _____ .

3. We both _____ .

How are you and Eduardo different?

4. Eduardo _____ , but I _____ .

5. Eduardo _____ , but I _____ .

6. Eduardo _____ , but I _____ .

GRAMMAR: ASK QUESTIONS

Be a Reporter

DIRECTIONS Write statements about yourself. Turn your statements into questions. Use *are*, *can*, and *do*.

Statements   **Questions**

1. I like to draw people.   Do you like to draw people?
    _____   _____

    _____   _____

2. _____   _____

    _____   _____

3. _____   _____

    _____   _____

4. _____   _____

    _____   _____

DIRECTIONS Ask a partner the questions. Write the answers.

_____

_____

_____

_____

_____

Could I Ask You a Question?
LEVEL A TE page T30

14

Unit 1 | Identity

RESEARCH SKILLS

Using a Map

DIRECTIONS Study the map. Label the map.
Use the words in the box.

river	city	country
lake	islands	ocean

South America

1. lake

GALAPAGOS ISLANDS

2.

3.

4.

5.

6.

FALKLAND ISLANDS

DIRECTIONS Answer the questions. Use the compass rose.

7. You are in Peru. You want to visit Brazil. In which direction do you go? _____

8. You are in Venezuela. You want to see Bolivia. In which direction do you go? _____

Explore Geography

DIRECTIONS Compare Puerto Rico and Miami. Use the Venn diagram.

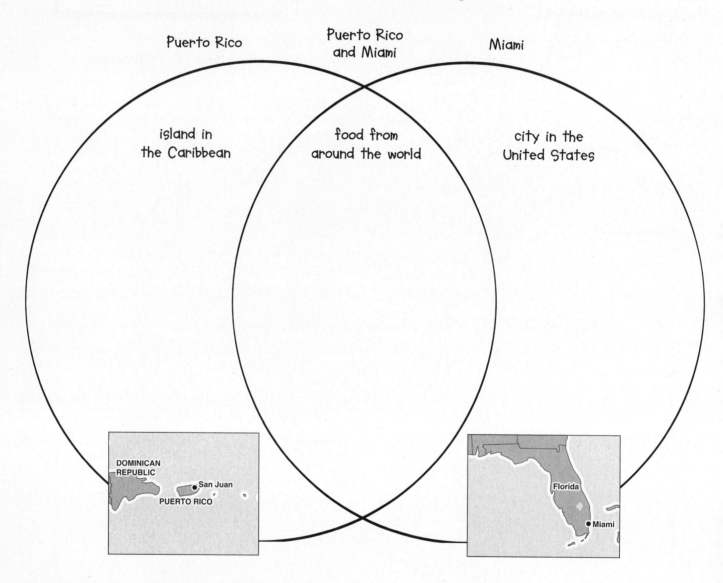

Puerto Rico

Puerto Rico
and Miami

Miami

island in
the Caribbean

food from
around the world

city in the
United States

DOMINICAN
REPUBLIC

• San Juan

PUERTO RICO

Florida

• Miami

DIRECTIONS Write two sentences that show how Puerto Rico and Miami are the same. Write two sentences that show how they are different.

1. _____

2. _____

3. _____

4. _____

Study a News Story

DIRECTIONS Work with a partner. Read the news story. Find each quotation. Write the quotation in the chart. Then write the question the writer probably asked.

Quotations and Questions

A **quotation** shows someone's exact words.

"It was pretty exciting!" said the worker.

Use these words to begin a **question**:

Is	Who	When
Are	Where	Why
Can	What	How
Do		

Lion Escapes From Zoo

A fourteen-year-old lion escaped from the city zoo today.

"We do not know how it got away," said a worker from the zoo.

"I'm afraid to go outside!" exclaimed a woman who lives near the zoo.

One zoo official said, "It might not be able to survive on its own."

A search and rescue team is looking for the lion. "We will catch it soon," said the leader of the team.

Workers do not know how this lion escaped from the zoo.

	Quotations	Questions
1.	"We do not know how it got away."	Do you know how the lion got away?
2.		
3.		
4.		

MORE ABOUT NEWS STORIES Think about a school event. Write questions about it. Then interview a partner. Write quotations to show your partner's answers.

BUILD LANGUAGE AND VOCABULARY

Brain Power at Work!

DIRECTIONS Read each sentence. Circle the correct present tense verb.

1. The students ___(prepare)/ **prepares**___ a report about Japan.

2. Mara ___**show / shows**___ word brain power.

3. She ___**read / reads**___ books about Japan.

4. Velina ___**like / likes**___ to talk.

5. She ___**ask / asks**___ questions about the country.

6. People ___**answer / answers**___ her questions.

7. The girls ___**write / writes**___ the report together.

8. Two boys ___**display / displays**___ artistic brain power.

9. They ___**draw / draws**___ maps and flags.

10. One boy ___**make / makes**___ a poster.

11. The poster ___**display / displays**___ pictures of Japan.

12. The pictures ___**show / shows**___ cities and gardens.

13. The four students ___**tell / tells**___ the class about Japan.

14. Japan ___**come / comes**___ alive for us!

JAPAN

Hokkaido

Sea of Japan

Honshu

Tokyo

Hiroshima

Shikoku

Kyushu

North Pacific Ocean

MORE ABOUT THE PRESENT TENSE Write sentences with present tense verbs. Tell how your friends use their brain power. Use the verbs *is* or *are* in some sentences.

Use Your Brain!

New Words

brain power

figure out

improve

intelligence

Use New Words in Context

DIRECTIONS Read the sentence starters. Draw lines to the words that can complete the sentences. Then write the sentences.

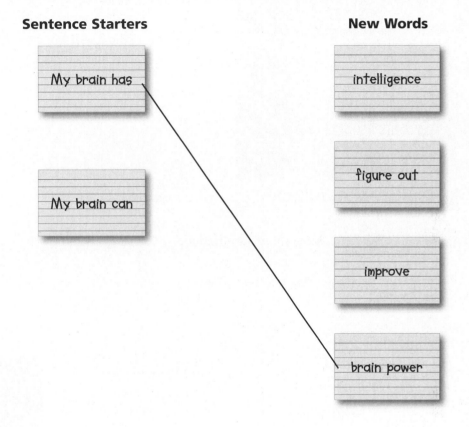

Sentence Starters

My brain has

My brain can

New Words

intelligence

figure out

improve

brain power

1. My brain has brain power. _____

2. _____

3. _____

4. _____

MORE ABOUT NEW WORDS Work with a partner. Write examples for each sentence.

Example:

My brain has brain power. I can think, learn, and move.

GRAMMAR: PRESENT TENSE

They Are Intelligent!

DIRECTIONS Work with a partner. Read each sentence. Write the correct verb.

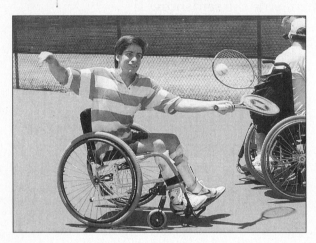

These athletes have movement intelligence.

<table>
<tr><td style="border: 1px solid black; padding: 10px;">Present Tense

A present tense verb tells what is happening now or what happens all the time.

   Athletes play tennis after school.

Add s to the verb to tell about one person, place, thing, or idea.

   Nico returns the ball.

Use a verb without s with I and you.

   I score a point.
   You play well.</td></tr>
</table>

1. The players _____use_____ movement intelligence.
   uses / use

2. They _____ their wheelchairs quickly.
   turn / turns

3. Each player _____ to win!
   want / wants

4. In sports, you _____ face-to-face intelligence, too.
   needs / need

5. You _____ with others.
   plays / play

6. The singer _____ musical intelligence.
   show / shows

7. She _____ on stage.
   sings / sing

8. I _____ to see her show.
   go / goes

9. The people _____ her music.
   love / loves

10. I _____ loudly with the audience.
    claps / clap

The singer performs with the group Sweet Harmony. She has musical intelligence.

MORE ABOUT THE PRESENT TENSE Tell a partner about your favorite singer or athlete. Have your partner listen for present tense verbs. Write them down in a list.

A Girl Works for Peace

Nadja Halilbegovich writes and sings. She also works for peace. What kinds of intelligence does she use?

Articles

An **article** helps identify a noun.

Use **a** or **an** to talk about one thing in a general way.

Use **a** before a consonant.
  I am reading about **a** girl.

Use **an** before a vowel.
  The girl is **an** author.

Use **the** to talk about one thing in a specific way.
  She is from **the** country of Bosnia.

DIRECTIONS Read each sentence. Circle the correct article.

1. Nadja Halilbegovich is ____the / (an)____ author.

2. Her diary tells about ____a / the____ problems in Bosnia.

3. She wants to help ____the / a____ world.

4. Nadja is also ____the / a____ singer.

5. She sings alone and with ____a / an____ choir.

DIRECTIONS Read each sentence. Circle the article. Then write *general* or *specific* on the line.

6. Today, Nadja lives in (the) United States.   ____specific____

7. She goes to a college in Indiana.   _____

8. She is a music student.   _____

9. Nadja is an activist.   _____

10. She tells the world about peace.   _____

MORE ABOUT ARTICLES Work with a partner. Write sentences to tell about an interesting person. Use the articles *a*, *an*, and *the*.

© Hampton-Brown

Make and Check Predictions

DIRECTIONS Follow the steps to make and check predictions.

1 Look at the picture and title.
Read the statements in the chart.
Write *T* for the true statements.
Write *F* for the false statements.

My Friend Has Many Intelligences!
by Oscar Hernandez

Before You Read	Statements About "My Friend Has Many Intelligences!"	After You Read
	Oscar's friend does not have musical intelligence.	
	He does not have movement intelligence.	
	He has artistic intelligence.	
	Oscar's friend has only two kinds of intelligence.	

2 Read about Oscar's friend.
Write *T* for the true statements.
Write *F* for the false statements.

> My friend Isaiah has many intelligences. He is good at sports. He plays on the tennis team. He has movement intelligence. He loves art class. He paints beautiful pictures. He has artistic intelligence. He sings in the school play. He has musical intelligence. My friend Isaiah has three kinds of intelligence!

3 Rewrite the false statements about Oscar's friend.
Make the statements true.

_____

_____

_____

22

Match Jobs and Skills

DIRECTIONS Learn about a job you can do. Follow the steps.

1 What job would you like to do? Circle one or add the name of a
new job to the list.

newspaper reporter	dancer	musician
graphic artist	doctor	_____
English teacher	architect	_____

2 Find out what skills you need for the job. Choose your sources.
Write the titles or names.

☐ book ☐ someone who has the job ☐ teacher ☐ other

_____   _____   _____   _____

_____   _____   _____   _____

3 Complete the diagram. Write the job and the skills you need for the job.
Then show which intelligence you need for each skill.

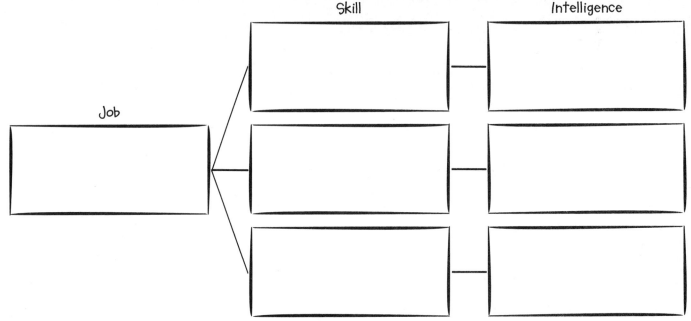

Skill   Intelligence

Job

4 Share the information with your class. Tell why the job is or is not
right for you.

What Kind? How Many?

DIRECTIONS Work with a partner. Read the description aloud to each other. Draw a circle around each adjective. Write each adjective in the correct column.

Adjectives

An **adjective** describes a person, place or thing.

Adjectives tell **what kind** or **how many**.

The artist paints **yellow** flowers. She paints on **four** walls.

A Spanish Courtyard

I enter an (old) courtyard in sunny Barcelona. I go in through a curved door in a high wall. The courtyard has an oval shape. Green vines cover the wall. A path leads from the door to a round fountain. (Colorful) tiles surround the fountain. I count thirty-six tiles. Two trees cast gray shadows on the ground. Four bushes grow nearby. They grow in the golden sunlight. A wooden bench sits beside one wall. It is a peaceful place.

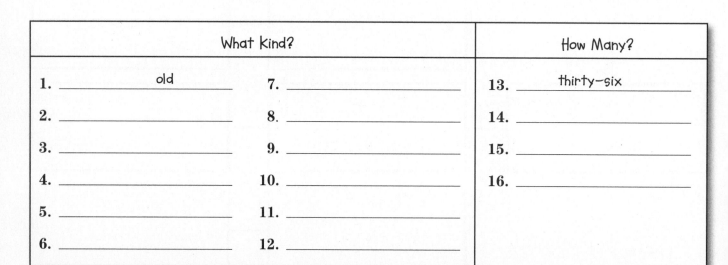

What Kind?		How Many?
1. ___old___	7. _____	13. __thirty-six__
2. _____	8. _____	14. _____
3. _____	9. _____	15. _____
4. _____	10. _____	16. _____
5. _____	11. _____	
6. _____	12. _____	

MORE ABOUT ADJECTIVES Draw a favorite place. Use sentences to describe it. Use adjectives from the chart or adjectives of your own.

LEARN KEY VOCABULARY

A Portrait Painter

New Words

accept

decide

express

feature

portrait

Use New Words in Context

DIRECTIONS Read each sentence. Circle the correct word. Then write the sentence.

1. I want to paint a ____ feature / (portrait) ____ of myself.

   I want to paint a portrait of myself.

2. I can ____ decide / accept ____ to use pencils or paints.

   _____

3. I can draw each ____ portrait / feature ____ , like my nose and eyes.

   _____

4. A picture is a way to ____ express / decide ____ my ideas.

   _____

5. I hope that my teacher will ____ decide / accept ____ my picture.

   _____

Use Context Clues

DIRECTIONS Complete the paragraph. Use the new words.

Miriam is an artist. She paints a ___ portrait ___ of herself. First, she
                                        6.

draws her face. Then, she draws all of its _____ . Miriam can
                                                   7.

_____ what colors to use. She chooses yellow and orange. Yellow
      8.

and orange _____ her happy feelings. She shows the painting to the
                  9.

judges. They like it! It looks like Miriam. They _____ it. Miriam's
                                                        10.

painting goes in the museum!

These Artists Create

DIRECTIONS Read each sentence. Circle the adjective.
Write *near* or *far*.

1. Look at (these) paintings on my wall. _____ *near* _____

2. That painting by the door is by

   Nancy Hom. _____

3. She drew those leaves. _____

4. Do you see this painting next to me? _____

5. George Littlechild painted these self-portraits. _____

Adjectives
The **adjectives** this, that, these, and those tell which one and how many.

	One	More Than One
Near	**This** pencil is in my hand.	**These** erasers are mine.
Far	**That** pencil is on your desk.	**Those** erasers are yours.

DIRECTIONS Read the conversation. Add the missing adjective.
Use *this*, *that*, *these*, or *those*.

Alex and Monica paint self-portraits. Alex picks up a paintbrush.

"Do you need _____ *this* _____ paintbrush?" he asks.
6.

"No," Monica says. "I don't need _____ one."
7.

Alex points to the paint on Monica's table. "Can you hand me _____
red paint?" 8.

Monica holds up two tubes of paint. "Do you like _____ colors?"
she asks. 9.

Alex shakes his head. "No. _____ colors are too dark."
10.

Monica holds up another tube. "Is _____ color better?"
11.

Alex nods. "Yes. _____ color is great. Thanks, Monica."
12.

MORE ABOUT ADJECTIVES Work with a partner. Act out the conversation
between Alex and Monica.

© Hampton-Brown

GRAMMAR: PROPER ADJECTIVES

A World of Artists

DIRECTIONS Read about each artist. Complete the chart. Use a proper adjective from the box.

> **Proper Adjectives**
>
> A **proper adjective** comes from a proper noun. It begins with a capital letter.
>
> **Italian** bread comes from Italy.

French	Spanish	Chinese	African
Vietnamese	Korean	Italian	English
Mexican	Japanese	Russian	American

Artist and Country of Birth	Kind of Art
1. Tran Tuyet-Mai, Vietnam	traditional _____Vietnamese_____ woodblock prints
2. Wang Wei, China	_____ poetry and paintings
3. Michelangelo, Italy	paintings on the ceiling of an _____ chapel
4. Georgia O'Keeffe, America	paintings of flowers and deserts in the _____ Southwest
5. Frida Kahlo, Mexico	self-portraits in _____ dress
6. Tensho Shubun, Japan	_____ ink paintings
7. John Constable, England	scenes of _____ country life
8. Berthe Morisot, France	paintings of _____ women and children
9. Diego Velázquez, Spain	portraits of _____ royalty
10. Liubov Popova, Russia	modern art in a _____ style

Relate Causes and Effects

DIRECTIONS Read the paragraph. Look for causes and effects.
Complete the chart.

Maya Christina Gonzalez

In my painting I show the light shining from my heart. The words around the border are things that I love, like polka dots and fire, and ways that I feel, like loud and hungry. I stuck paintbrushes and pencils in my hair because I wanted to look good for my picture. The whole picture is lopsided because that's how it came out of the copy machine and I like it that way! Some of my best paintings happen by accident. You just never know.

Self-Portrait, Maya Christina Gonzalez, acrylics. Copyright ©1997.

Causes	Effects
Maya loves polka dots and fire.	
	She wrote "loud" and "hungry" on the border of her painting.
She wanted to look good for her picture.	
	Her self-portrait is lopsided.

DIRECTIONS Write sentences. Use a cause and an effect. Use the word *because*.

Example: Maya stuck paintbrushes and pencils in her hair because she wanted
to look good for her picture.

1. _____

   _____

2. _____

   _____

GRAMMAR: NOUNS

Off to New York!

DIRECTIONS Read the poem. Choose nouns from the box to complete the sentences.

Common and Proper Nouns

A **common noun** names any person, place or thing.

My **aunt** is in the **city**.

A **proper noun** names a particular person, place, or thing. It begins with a capital letter.

Aunt Mae is in **New York**.

A noun is often the subject of a sentence.

The **train** arrives at noon.

Tuesday in the City

Malia wants to be an _____actor_____ .
1.

New York is the _____ to be.
2.

The _____ are fantastic!
3.

The _____ are great to see.
4.

Her _____ makes an offer.
5.

"On _____ we'll go to a play.
6.

The train is only a _____
from my house.   7.

Come with me for the _____ !"
8.

day	place	actor
Tuesday	mile	shows
theaters	Aunt Mae	

DIRECTIONS Circle all the nouns in the poem. Then write each noun in the correct column.

Common Nouns		Proper Nouns
9. _actor_	14. _____	19. _____
10. _____	15. _____	20. _____
11. _____	16. _____	21. _____
12. _____	17. _____	22. _____
13. _____	18. _____	

WRITING: A SELF-PORTRAIT

All About You!

DIRECTIONS Follow the steps to create a self-portrait.

1 Draw a picture of yourself. Write words that tell about you.

Self-Portrait

A **self-portrait** can be a drawing you make of yourself. It can also be sentences you write that tell what you are like. A **self-portrait** describes who you are.

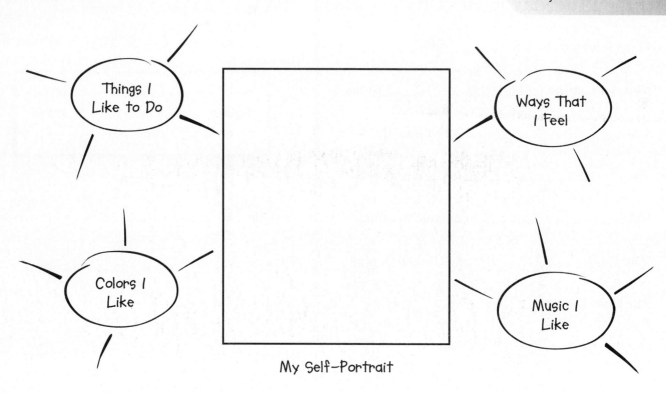

My Self-Portrait

2 Use the web to write sentences.

1. I like to _____

   because _____ .

2. I feel _____

   because _____ .

3. I like the colors _____

   because _____ .

4. My favorite music is _____

   because _____ .

3 Share your self-portrait with the class. Add it to the portrait gallery.

CONTENT AREA CONNECTIONS

Research a Portrait Artist

DIRECTIONS Find out about an artist. Use the information to complete the notecards. Use the notecards for your oral report. They can help you remember what to say.

About the Artist's Life

The artist's name is

The artist was born in the year

The artist lived in

One interesting thing about the artist is

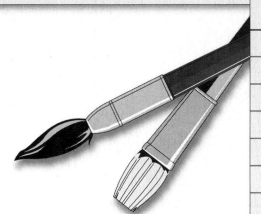

The Artist's Work

The artist made

The artist liked to use

One interesting thing about the artist's work is

What I Like About the Art

The art I like is called

I like it because

UNIT 2 MIND MAP

Cooperation

DIRECTIONS Use the mind map to write about cooperation. Read each selection in this unit. Add to the map ideas you learn about cooperation.

Looks Like	Sounds Like	Feels Like

Tell How They Work Together

DIRECTIONS Read the sentences. Write the correct pronouns.

> **Subject Pronouns**
>
> A pronoun takes the place of a noun. A **subject pronoun** tells who does something.
>
> **Hannah** works hard.
>
> **She** works hard.

Subject Pronouns

One	More Than One
I	we
you	you
he, she, it	they

They work together.

1. **The men and women** work together. _____They_____ build a barn.

2. **One man** gets people started. _____ calls out, "Lift!"

3. **The frame** for the barn is in the air. _____ is very heavy.

4. **Abigail** helps her mother. _____ carries things from the house.

5. **My friend and I** watch from the road. _____ offer to help.

DIRECTIONS Write subject pronouns to complete the passage.

Anna and Jamil work on a report. _____It_____ is about the Amish
6.

people. _____ want to do a good job. Jamil does research on the
7.

Internet. _____ likes to work on computers.
8.

Anna turns to Jamil. "_____ do that part," she says.
9.

"_____ want to go to the library. _____ has lots of books."
10.   **11.**

"Okay," says Jamil. "That way _____ can get lots of information."
12.

Words About Teamwork

New Words

care for

cooperate

depend on

member

plan

proud

solve problems

team

Relate Words

DIRECTIONS Use the new words to complete the web.

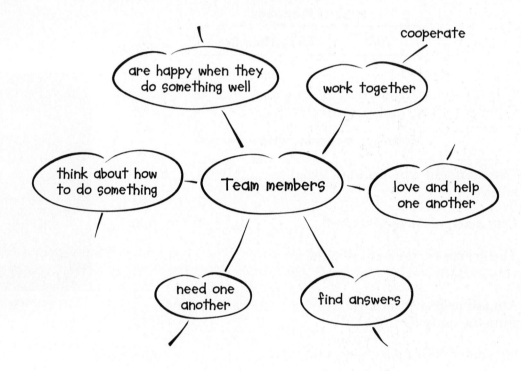

Use New Words in Context

DIRECTIONS Work with a partner. Write sentences about team members. Use the new words.

1. Team members _____care for each other_____ .

2. They _____ .

3. Team members _____ .

4. They _____ .

5. They feel _____ .

6. They _____ .

7. Each person is a _____ .

8. They _____ .

GRAMMAR: COUNT AND NONCOUNT NOUNS

Teamwork Saves Lives!

DIRECTIONS Underline all the nouns in the passage. Then write each noun where it belongs in the chart. Look on Handbook pages 410–411 for help.

In an <u>emergency</u>, people work together. First someone calls 911. The 911 operator gets <u>information</u> about the accident. Then she calls the police, firefighters, or paramedics.

The team comes in an ambulance. Sometimes they drive through rain or fog. They bring lots of equipment. They get the person to the hospital in time.

The doctors put on special clothing. They use their knowledge to help the patient recover.

Count and Noncount Nouns

A noun names a person, place, thing, or idea. A **count noun** names something you can count.

  1 nurse   2 nurses

A **noncount noun** names something you cannot count.

  equipment   health

Count Nouns	Noncount Nouns
1. _____emergency_____	13. _____information_____
2. _____	14. _____
3. _____	15. _____
4. _____	16. _____
5. _____	17. _____
6. _____	18. _____
7. _____	19. _____
8. _____	20. _____
9. _____	
10. _____	
11. _____	
12. _____	

Identify Main Ideas

DIRECTIONS Read the news article. Write key words and important ideas in the chart.

Big Game Tonight!

The Lincoln Lions meet the Whitman Whirlwinds on the basketball court tonight. The Lions are a good team. They are well-prepared. Everyone expects them to win.

"I am very proud of this team," says coach Green. "The girls work together. No one tries to be the star. They cooperate."

Green is right. Each player is respected. Each player is important. They depend on one another. Teamwork wins games!

The Lions use teamwork to win games.

Paragraph	Key Words	Important Ideas
1	good team,	
2		
3		

DIRECTIONS Finish the paragraph. Use the important ideas from your chart.

The Lincoln Lions are a good team. The players _____

_____

_____

_____

GRAMMAR: SUBJECT PRONOUNS

They Are a Team

DIRECTIONS Read the sentences. Write the correct pronouns.

1. **My friend and I** see a team of oxen. _____We_____ watch the oxen work.

2. **The oxen** work together. _____ pull the plow.

3. **Mr. Davidov** guides the plow. _____ steers it.

4. **The plow** loosens the soil. _____ digs into the hard earth.

5. **The field** is bare now. _____ is ready for seeds.

6. **Sofia and Eva** are a team. _____ plant the seeds.

7. **Sofia** has some seeds. _____ drops the seeds into the ground.

8. Sofia tells **Eva**, "Take a rest. _____ are tired."

> ### Subject Pronouns
> A pronoun takes the place of a noun. A **subject pronoun** tells who does something.
>
> **The oxen** pull the plow.
> ↓
> **They** pull the plow.

Subject Pronouns

One	More Than One
I	we
you	you
he, she, it	they

DIRECTIONS Write sentences about the picture. Use subject pronouns.

He steers the plow. _____

_____

_____

_____

_____

_____

_____

Take Notes

DIRECTIONS Take notes to answer a question about a topic. Follow the steps.

1 Read the article. Look for answers to the question: **What work does each type of honeybee do?**

> **How to Take Notes**
>
> **Notes** are important words, phrases, and ideas you write down as you read. The notes help you remember and organize information. To take notes, use your own words. Use quotation marks when you copy exactly what you read.

Honeybees Work as a Team

Honeybees live in a hive.

Honeybees live in a hive. There are three types of bees in a hive.

The Queen The queen is the largest bee in the colony. She is the only bee in the hive that lays eggs. The queen can lay up to 3,000 eggs in one day. The hive would not survive without the queen.

The Drones Drones are male bees. They have no stingers. Drones do not collect food or pollen. They mate with the queen.

The Workers Workers feed the queen and young bees. They guard the hive. They fan their wings to keep it cool. Worker bees also collect nectar to make honey. 60,000 workers may live in a hive.

---

2 Take notes. Complete the notecard. Use the details from the article. Do your notes answer the research question?

Notecard

Research Question	What work does each type of honeybee do?
Source	www.honey.com/kids
Notes	queen:
	drones:
	workers:
Quotation	

3 Review your notes. What did you find out about honeybees? Share the information with your class.

© Hampton-Brown

Research a Team

DIRECTIONS Follow the steps to research a wildlife team.

1 Choose a wildlife team. Answer the questions.

- What team will I study? _____ _____

- What information do I need to know? _____

  _____

- Where will I look for information?
  ☐ book   ☐ encyclopedia   ☐ Internet

  _____   _____   _____

  _____   _____   _____

2 Take notes. Write important words, phrases, and ideas. Remember to use your own words. Look on Handbook page 369 for help.

3 Organize your ideas. Use your notes to complete the chart.

Team: _____

A Group is Called	Number of Members	What the Team Does

4 Write sentences about your team. Add pictures. Share them with your class.

Attach a picture of your wildlife team here.	_____
	_____
	_____
	_____

BUILD LANGUAGE AND VOCABULARY

Sunday Is Tamale Day

DIRECTIONS Read each sentence. Circle the possessive pronouns.

1. (My) family visits together in our kitchen.

2. The family loves the kitchen with its food and wonderful smells.

3. Mother makes her tamales on Sundays.

4. My uncles and aunts bring their children to help.

5. Our grandmother always wears her best apron.

6. All the relatives wrap the tamales with their hands.

7. Grandfather tells his best stories then.

8. Does your family visit around the kitchen table?

> **Possessive Pronouns**
>
> A pronoun takes the place of a noun. A **possessive pronoun** shows who or what owns something.
>
> This is Mama's kitchen.
> That is **her** stove.

Possessive Pronouns

One	More Than One
my	our
your	your
his, her, its	their

Reprinted with permission of the publisher, Children's Book Press, San Francisco, CA. Copyright © 1990 by Carmen Lomas Garza.

DIRECTIONS Write sentences about your family. Use possessive pronouns. Share your sentences with a partner.

_____

_____

_____

_____

_____

_____

Words to Build By

New Words

- adobe
- bar
- entire
- gather
- layer
- plaster
- reality
- require
- tend
- weathered

Use Definitions

DIRECTIONS Work with a partner. Read each sentence.
Mark *T* for true. Mark *F* for false.

___F___ **1.** An **adobe** is a brick made of cement.

_____ **2.** A **weathered** brick is changed by the wind, sun, and rain.

_____ **3.** To **gather** means to come together.

_____ **4.** Something **entire** is broken or incomplete.

_____ **5.** A **layer** is one thickness of something.

_____ **6.** **Reality** is the same thing as a dream.

_____ **7.** To **tend** something is to take care of it.

_____ **8.** A **bar** is as wide as it is long.

_____ **9.** You can **plaster** a wall to protect it.

_____**10.** When you **require** something, you need it.

Use New Words in Context

DIRECTIONS Work with a partner. Answer the questions.
Use complete sentences.

11. What is a **bar** of **adobe** made of? _A bar of adobe is made of mud._

_____

12. Why do you need to **plaster** a new **layer** on a **weathered** house? _____

_____

13. Why is it better when an **entire** family can **gather** to help? _____

_____

14. What tools do you **require** when you **tend** a garden? _____

_____

15. How can you make a dream become **reality**? _____

_____

LITERARY ANALYSIS: SIMILE

Like Flowers in a Garden

DIRECTIONS Find each simile. Underline it. Write the two things the simile compares.

> **Simile**
> A **simile** compares two things.
> Some similes use the word *like*:
> Jon swims **like a fish.**
> Some similes use the word *as*:
> Ann is **as busy as a bee.**

1. Adobes are <u>like big chocolate bars</u>.

adobes, chocolate bars _____

2. The family works together like bees in a hive. _____

3. The roses are as red as a stop sign. _____

4. The grass in the yard is as green as a frog. _____

5. Papi works in the garden like an ox. _____

6. The sun shines on the garden like a smile. _____

DIRECTIONS Look at the two pictures. Answer the questions. Use a simile.

pond

ice cube

sunflower

man

7. How cold is the pond?

The pond is as cold as an ice cube. _____

9. How tall is the sunflower?

_____

_____

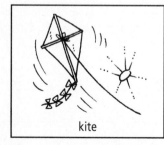
kite

bird

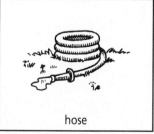
snake   hose

8. How does the kite fly?

_____

_____

10. How does the snake coil?

_____

_____

© Hampton-Brown

More Than One

DIRECTIONS Complete each sentence. Use the plural form of a noun from the box.

star	fox	bike
waltz	family	rosebush
glass	wish	night
story	porch	bug

Plural Nouns

Plural nouns name more than one person, place, thing, or idea.

Add **-s** to most nouns.

aunts   adobes   dreams

For nouns that end in **x, ch, sh, s,** or **z,** add **-es.**

boxes   lunches   bushes

For nouns that end in a **consonant** plus **y,** change **y** to **i** and add **-es.**

comedies   cities   skies

1. In my neighborhood, we gather together on warm _____nights_____ .

2. The parents sit on the _____ and talk.

3. They drink _____ of ice water.

4. The grandparents smell the perfume of the _____ .

5. They tell _____ from long ago.

6. They remember _____ and other dances.

7. The little boys and girls play like young _____ .

8. The older kids ride their _____ .

9. My friends and I look for crickets and other _____ .

10. Sometimes, we share our hopes and _____ for the future.

11. We all watch the sky for shiny _____ .

12. Our _____ have a nice time together.

MORE ABOUT NOUNS Work with a partner. Look around the room for more people, places, or things. Make a chart of the nouns and their plurals.

Name ______________________ Date ______________

SUM IT UP

Visualize

DIRECTIONS Read the poem. Which words help you make a picture in your mind? Underline the words. Then draw what you see.

Winter Tide

— Kellie Crain

Silver light falls
through dark clouds
to hit the shore.
Icy waves bite at the rocks.
The sea spits sharp, salty drops
that glitter in the moonlight.

DIRECTIONS Share your picture with a partner. Complete the sentences.

1. I underlined the words ______________________.
2. My partner underlined the words ______________________.
3. My picture shows ______________________.
4. My partner's picture shows ______________________.

GRAMMAR: PREPOSITIONAL PHRASES

In the Shade of the Trees

DIRECTIONS Read each sentence. Add a preposition. Then read the sentence again. Does it makes sense?

Prepositional Phrases

A **preposition** can show location, direction, or time.

Leaves blow **across** the yard.

A preposition is the first word in a **prepositional phrase**. Prepositional phrases add details to sentences.

Mami plants seeds **near the path**.

Some Prepositions

Location	Time	Direction
in	until	through
behind	before	into
on	during	around
under	after	from
next to	at	across

1. Juan and I make bricks _____under_____ a big tree.

2. The tree is _____ the house.

3. Mami watches _____ the window.

4. She cooks beans _____ the stove.

5. We put the bricks _____ the sun to dry.

6. The sun is hot _____ the day.

7. Juan and I eat lunch _____ noon.

8. We sit _____ the tree.

9. At 6:00, Papi comes _____ the gate.

10. He walks _____ the yard.

11. He steps _____ the adobe bricks.

12. He is tired _____ his day at work.

13. He left for work _____ dawn.

14. We all relax inside the house _____ bedtime.

15. Then we settle _____ our warm, soft beds.

Read It to Me

DIRECTIONS Use object pronouns. Complete the conversation.

> **Object Pronouns**
>
> A **pronoun** takes the place of a noun. Use an **object pronoun** after a preposition or a verb.
>
> Give the **glasses** to Khen.
>
> Khen uses **them** to read.

Object Pronouns

One	More Than One
me	us
you	you
him, her, it	them

1. I like this book. Can you read it to ____me____ ?

2. I need my **glasses**. Please bring _____ to me.

3. Your **glasses** are up too high. I cannot reach _____ .

4. Use the **stool**. You can reach my glasses with _____ .

5. I see **Chang** is here. Can you read to _____ , too?

6. Yes. I think the story is **Chang's** favorite. I'll read _____ to both of you.

7. Good. You can share the book with **Chang and me**. Please read to _____ .

8. Sit down, **Chang**. I can sit beside _____ . **Huong** is on the rug. You can sit beside _____ .

© Hampton-Brown

Words About Cooperation

New Words

blind

command

count on

guide dog

instructor

partner

personality

skill

take care of

training

Relate Words

DIRECTIONS Complete each sentence. Use an ending from the box.

> training to the team   a gentle personality
>
> to be a helpful partner   every command
>
> take care of a blind person

1. A guide dog must learn how to _take care of a blind person_____ .

2. A guide dog has special skills and _____ .

3. Dogs must learn to obey _____ .

4. An instructor gives the _____ .

5. You can count on a guide dog _____ .

Use New Words in Context

DIRECTIONS Work with a partner. Write sentences about cooperation. Use each new word below.

6. take care of _____

   _____

7. training _____

   _____

8. count on _____

   _____

9. skills _____

   _____

10. blind _____

   _____

Their Dogs Work Hard

DIRECTIONS Read each sentence. Write a possessive pronoun to replace the words in bold.

> **Possessive Pronouns**
>
> A **possessive pronoun** tells who or what owns something.
>
> This is **Anne's** dog.
> ↓
> This is **her** dog.

Possessive Pronouns

One	More Than One
my	our
your	your
his, her, its	their

1. The teachers meet **the teachers'** students.   _their_

2. Stacy is a trainer. Stacy meets **Stacy's** new student.   _____

3. The student is a boy. **The boy's** name is Moe.   _____

4. Stacy tells Moe, "I am **Moe's** teacher."   _____

5. "Thank you for being **Moe's** teacher," says Moe.   _____

DIRECTIONS Complete the passage. Use possessive pronouns.

Gita works at the Guide Dog Training Center. She teaches the students and ___their___
6.

dogs. "Hi, Rob," she says. "Here is _____ dog. _____ name is Cera."
                                        7.   8.

Rob pets _____ dog. "Hello, Cera," he says. "You are _____ dog now."
          9.   10.

Gita brings a dog to a girl named Chucha. _____ dog is named Ginger.
                                              11.

Gita gives Rob and Chucha directions. "Tell _____ dogs to 'sit.' Then put on
                                                12.

_____ leashes."
    13.

Rob and Chucha help _____ dogs. "We are ready," Chucha says. "Let's take
                        14.

_____ dogs for a walk!"
    15.

© Hampton-Brown

Identify Steps in a Process

DIRECTIONS Make a storyboard about Moe and Aria.

1 **Put the Events in Order** Write them on the storyboard. Draw a picture of each event.

> Moe and Aria learn skills.   Stacy chooses Aria to be Moe's partner.
>
> Moe and Aria go home together.   Moe goes to the training center.

2 **Make a Prediction** Show what you think will happen to Moe and Aria next. Add pictures and sentences to the storyboard.

3 **Share Your Storyboard** Talk about your storyboard with a partner.

Storyboard About Moe and Aria

1. Moe goes to the training center.	2. _____
3. _____	4. _____
5. _____	6. _____

GRAMMAR: OBJECT PRONOUNS

You Can Count on Them

DIRECTIONS What words can replace each object pronoun? Choose words from the box. Write them in the chart.

the boy	Moe and Aria	Moe
the dog	the girl	the students
the elevator	Stacy	the blind man
the dogs	the bank	the woman

> **Object Pronouns**
>
> An **object pronoun** can follow a verb.
>   Mathias brushes **the dog**.
>   ↓
>   Mathias brushes **it**.
>
> An object pronoun can also follow a preposition.
>   The dog runs to **Jim and Phan**.
>   ↓
>   The dog runs to **them**.

Give the dog to **him**.	Take the dog to **her**.	Learn about **it**.	You can help **them**.
1. _the boy_ ____	4. _____	7. _____	10. _Moe and Aria_
2. _____	5. _____	8. _____	11. _____
3. _____	6. _____	9. _____	12. _____

DIRECTIONS Read part of Alma's letter. Circle the correct object pronouns.

Dear Papi,

I am very busy at the Guide Dog Training Center. I want ___him /(you)___ to meet my
                                                              13.

dog! I feed and brush ___it / them___ every day. It sleeps next to ___you / me___ . Phan is
                              14.   15.

our trainer. She teaches ___her / us___ to work together.
                                 16.

I have a friend named Ali. I eat breakfast with ___him / it___ . Tomorrow, we take our
                                                        17.

dogs to the park. We can walk with ___him / them___ .
                                           18.

WRITING: A THANK-YOU LETTER

Thanks for Everything!

A Thank-You Letter

A **thank-you letter** thanks someone for doing something nice. It has a **heading**, a **greeting**, a **body**, a **closing**, and a **signature**.

DIRECTIONS Write a thank-you letter. Choose one of these ideas.

• You are Moe. Thank Stacy for training Aria or helping you learn how to use a guide dog.

• You are Stacy. Thank Moe for coming to the center.

In the **heading**, write your address and today's date.

_____

_____

_____

Write the **greeting**. Write *Dear* and the person's name.

Dear _____ ,

Thank you for _____

_____

_____

_____

Write the **body**. Say "thank you." Tell how you feel about what the person did. Use words like *I appreciate* and *I'm so grateful*.

_____

_____

_____

_____

Write a **closing** like *Sincerely, Yours truly,* or *Your friend.* Then write your name. That is your **signature**.

_____ ,

_____

Using the Internet

DIRECTIONS Work with your team. Use the Internet to find information.

1 **Plan Your Research** Think about what you will do. Finish the sentences.

- Our topic is _____ .

- Our research question is _____

  _____ .

- Here are some key words we can use: _____

  _____

2 **Use the Internet** Use the key words to look up information.
See Handbook pages 364–365 for help.

3 **Take Notes** Complete a chart as you use the Internet.

Web site	Notes

Did the Web sites help you find information to answer your research question?

☐ yes   ☐ no   If you checked "no," try more Web sites.

4 **Explain Results** Tell the class what you learned. Be ready to answer
these questions.

- What was your research question? What answers did you find?

- Which Web site did you use? What did you like about it?

Just Ask Me

Questions and Statements

A **question** asks something.
Who needs help?

A **statement** tells something.
The man needs help.

DIRECTIONS Study the chart. Add one more thing
to each category.

What Do People Need to Survive?

shelter	water	food	health
house	to drink	grains	love
tent	to water crops	vegetables	safety
houseboat	to cook	meat	exercise

DIRECTIONS Ask for and give information. Write a question or a statement
to complete each item. Use the chart above for ideas. Add ideas of your own.

1. _Why do people need water?_____

   People need water to drink and to water crops.

2. Where can people find shelter?

   _____

3. What kinds of food do people need to eat?

   _____

4. _____

   People need love, safety, and exercise to stay healthy.

MORE ABOUT QUESTIONS AND STATEMENTS Work with a partner. Ask and answer
questions of your own.

Action Words

New Words

answer

brave

climb

hold on

lower

pull

remove

silence

tighten

weight

Sort Words

DIRECTIONS Study the new words. Write the new words where they belong in the chart.

Words That Show Action	Words That Do Not Show Action
climb	brave

Rock climbers

Use New Words in Context

DIRECTIONS Work with a group. Write a sentence for each new word.

1. _Alicia is a brave person._____

2. _____

3. _____

4. _____

5. _____

6. _____

7. _____

8. _____

9. _____

10. _____

GRAMMAR: REFLEXIVE PRONOUNS

Keep Yourself Safe!

DIRECTIONS Read each noun. Draw a line to the reflexive pronoun.

Nouns	Reflexive Pronouns
1. the father	myself
2. the rescue dog	yourself
3. the girl	himself
4. me	herself
5. you	ourselves
6. you and your friend	yourselves
7. me and my friend	itself
8. the climbers	themselves

> **Reflexive Pronouns**
> To talk about someone twice in a sentence, use a **reflexive pronoun**. A reflexive pronoun refers to the subject.
>
> He can not save **himself**.
>
> The rescuers **themselves** are worried.

DIRECTIONS Complete the article. Add reflexive pronouns from the box.

Local Heroes

"Hikers often get hurt," say Kichi and Eddie. "We rescue them

_____ourselves_____ ."
      9.

"We teach hikers not to hike alone," adds Eddie. "It's dangerous.

Eddie and Kichi Arimoto

I never do it _____ ."
      10.

"That's true," says Kichi. "You might hurt _____ . Could a boy with a
      11.

broken leg get home by _____ ? I don't think so."
      12.

Eddie and Kichi train _____ . Kichi teaches _____ basic
      13.   **14.**

first aid and CPR. Eddie takes classes.

GRAMMAR: POSSESSIVE NOUNS

A Family's Hike

DIRECTIONS Read each sentence. Circle the correct possessive noun.

1. _____(Michael's)/ Michaels'_____ family likes to hike.

2. They ride in his ___mother's / mothers'___ car.

3. They look at his ___father's / fathers'___ maps.

4. They stop the ___car's / cars'___ engine.

5. They find his ___parent's / parents'___ favorite trail.

DIRECTIONS Rewrite each sentence. Use a possessive noun to replace the word in parentheses.

6. The mother checks the (boy) gear.

   The mother checks the boy's gear.

7. (Dad) backpack is full of healthy snacks.

   _____

8. The (water bottles) lids are tight.

   _____

9. The (parents) equipment is ready.

   _____

10. The (family) hike begins.

   _____

> **Possessive Nouns**
>
> A **possessive noun** is the name of an owner. The name always has an apostrophe: '.
>
> Add **'s** if the noun names one owner.
>   the climber's rope
>
> Add **'** if the noun names more than one owner and ends with **s**.
>   the hikers' safety
>
> Add **'s** if the noun is plural and doesn't end with **s**.
>   the children's backpacks

MORE ABOUT POSSESSIVE NOUNS Talk about items in your classroom with a partner. Use possessive nouns.

Example:
Adela has a pen.
It is Adela's pen.

The teachers share a computer.
It is the teachers' computer.

Identify Problems and Solutions

DIRECTIONS Read the story. Complete the chart. Then use your chart to retell the story to a partner.

Doc to the Rescue!

Jeff Ecklund likes to ski. One day, an avalanche sends ice and snow down the mountain. In seconds, Jeff is trapped under 5 feet of ice!

A rescue team sets out. Dave Paradysz brings a dog named Doc. The dog finds Jeff's scent. He thumps the snow. He wags his tail and starts to dig.

Jeff is under the snow. He is hurt. He cannot move or get out. Then something touches his back. It is Doc's paw. Jeff is saved!

Rescuers dig Jeff out. He is safe. After three months, he can ski again.

Doc saved Jeff's life.

Problem and Solution Chart

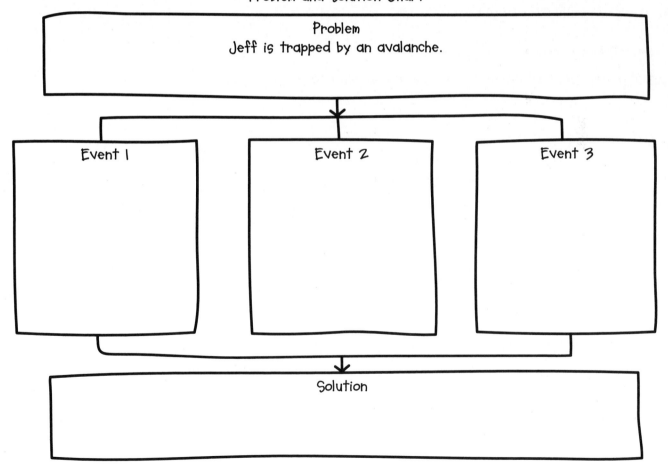

Problem
Jeff is trapped by an avalanche.

Event 1

Event 2

Event 3

Solution

GRAMMAR: SUBJECT AND OBJECT PRONOUNS

Thanks! You Helped Us!

DIRECTIONS Read the sentences. Circle each pronoun. Tell which kind of pronoun it is.

Subject and Object Pronouns

A **pronoun** takes the place of a noun.

A **subject pronoun** tells who or what does something.

The man is in trouble.
He needs help.

An **object pronoun** follows a verb or a preposition.

Camila helps the man.
Camila rescues him.

Subject Pronouns

One	More Than One
I	we
you	you
he, she, it	they

Object Pronouns

One	More Than One
me	us
you	you
him, her, it	them

1. Camila is a rescue worker. (She) gets a call for help.   _subject_

2. A hiker is hurt. He needs help.   _____

3. Camila's team goes to him.   _____

4. They lower Camila down on a rope.   _____

5. The team pulls them both up.   _____

DIRECTIONS Read the thank–you note. Circle the correct pronouns.

December 10, 2002

Dear Camila,

Thank ___**they /** (**you**)___ for all your help. Hikers fall, and you rescue ___**they / them**___ .
     6.   7.

I like your teammate, Katrina. ___**She / Her**___ makes me laugh. I like Shabbir, too.
                                8.

___**He / Him**___ is very strong. Please thank ___**he / him**___ for me. All of your teammates are
    9.   10.

very brave. Do ___**they / them**___ always work together so well?
             11.

My family is very grateful. ___**We / Us**___ are all thankful for your help. My sister wants to
                    12.

meet ___**you / us**___ . Please visit ___**we / us**___ soon.
    13.   14.

Sincerely,

Sergio Villa

Use Map Skills

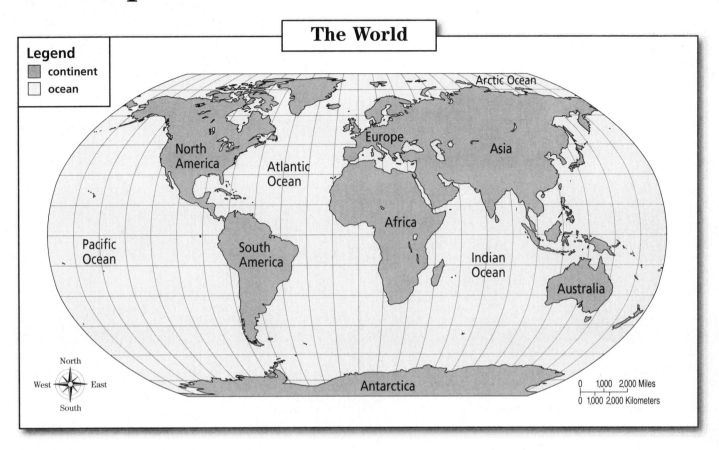

The World

Legend
- continent
- ocean

North America
Atlantic Ocean
Arctic Ocean
Europe
Asia
Africa
Indian Ocean
Pacific Ocean
South America
Australia
Antarctica

North
West — East
South

0   1,000   2,000 Miles
0   1,000   2,000 Kilometers

DIRECTIONS Study the world map. Then read each sentence.
Circle the correct word.

1. South America is a ___continent / ocean___ .

2. Asia is a ___continent / ocean___ .

3. Europe is ___north / south___ of Africa.

4. Use a scale for ___direction / distance___ .

5. North America is ___east / west___ of Europe.

6. Australia is a ___ocean / continent___ .

7. Australia is ___south / north___ of Asia.

8. The distance from South America to Africa
   is ___2000 / 6000___ miles.

9. The Indian Ocean is ___east / west___
   of the Atlantic Ocean.

10. Asia is ___north / south___ of the
    Arctic Ocean.

MORE ABOUT MAPS Talk with a partner. Ask and answer questions
about the world.

Example:
What ocean is west of Australia?
The Indian Ocean is west of Australia.

Explore Geography

DIRECTIONS Follow the steps to create a map of the Alps.

1 Study the map. Use it to answer the questions.

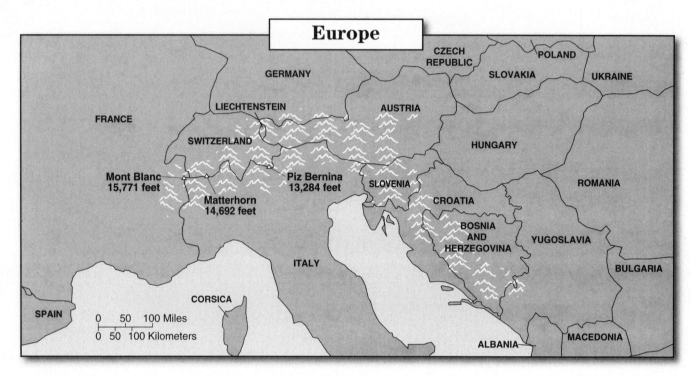

1. What countries do the Alps pass through? _____

_____

2. How long are the Alps? _____

3. How wide are the Alps? _____

4. What is the tallest mountain? _____

   How tall is it? _____

2 Use your answers to help you make a map of the Alps.

 • Choose your materials:

   ☐ clay   ☐ felt   ☐ papier-mâché   ☐ computer graphics   ☐ other _____

 • Make a fact sheet. Include this information:

   ☐ length of Alps   ☐ height of Alps   ☐ tallest mountains

3 Share your map and fact sheet with the class.

CONTENT AREA CONNECTIONS

Compare Mountains

DIRECTIONS Work with a group. Follow the steps to study a mountain.

1 **Choose a Topic** Circle the mountain your group will study.

Aconcagua	Elbrus	Puncak Jaya
Kilimanjaro	Everest	Vinson Massif
McKinley		

Mount Elbrus, Russia

2 **Find Sources** Check the sources you use. Write the titles or names.

☐ encyclopedia   ☐ atlas   ☐ Internet   ☐ other

_____   _____   _____   _____

_____   _____   _____   _____

_____   _____   _____   _____

3 **Take Notes** Complete the chart.

Name of the Mountain	Continent and Country	Height	Date First Climbed	Interesting Details

4 **Share Information** Add facts about your mountain to a class chart. Talk about how the mountains are the same and how they are different.

UNIT 3 MIND MAP

Relationships

DIRECTIONS Use the mind map to write about your relationships. Then read each selection in this unit. Add to the map ideas you learn about relationships.

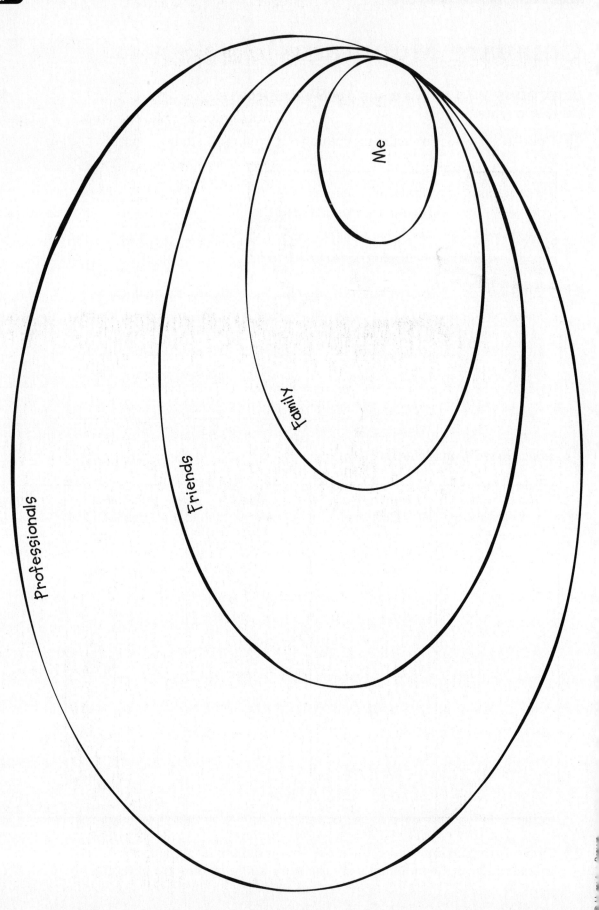

Me

Family

Friends

Professionals

BUILD LANGUAGE AND VOCABULARY

A Feeling of Friendship

DIRECTIONS Write the past tense form of the verb in parentheses.

Past Tense

A **past tense verb** tells about an action that happened earlier, or in the past. Most past tense verbs end in **–ed**.

> The friends **walked** home.
> They **joked** along the way.
> They **skipped** to the store.
> They **studied** all night.

1. Hector's family _____moved_____ in next door. (**move**)

2. My mother _____ them a cake. (**bake**)

3. I _____ it to Hector's house. (**carry**)

4. Hector and I _____ a football game. (**watch**)

5. We _____ for the same team. (**clap**)

6. We _____ outside to play ball. (**hurry**)

7. His dog _____ his tail at me. (**wag**)

8. Hector's whole family _____ nice to me. (**seem**)

DIRECTIONS How did your friendship with someone begin? Draw pictures in the flow chart. Write a sentence to go with each picture. Use a verb from the box. Change the verb to the past tense.

Some Verbs			
share	smile	wave	hop
talk	laugh	play	cry
study	stop	help	hurry

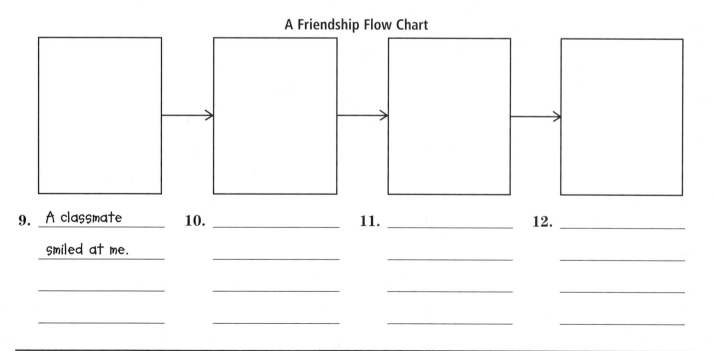

A Friendship Flow Chart

9. _A classmate_   10. _____   11. _____   12. _____

smiled at me.   _____   _____   _____

_____   _____   _____   _____

_____   _____   _____   _____

Friendship Words

New Words
dance
jealous
kindness
show off
terrified
trap

Relate Words

DIRECTIONS Write the new word that goes with each group of words.

1. move in a quick and lively way, move your body

   to music, _____dance_____

2. helpfulness, a good thing you do or say, _____

3. a bad feeling, wanting what someone else has, _____

4. a net or a cage, something used to catch an animal, _____

5. show how well you do something, get attention, _____

6. scared, frightened, _____

Use New Words in Context

DIRECTIONS Read each sentence. Add the best new word to complete the sentence.

7. My friend and I decided to sing and _____dance_____ in a contest.

8. She was not scared, but I was _____ .

9. I felt like an animal caught in a _____ !

10. She began to _____ her dance steps for the judges.

11. I felt _____ when she won first prize.

12. The judges showed _____ and gave me a prize for my singing.

MORE ABOUT NEW WORDS Work with a partner. Write sentences about friendship. Use a new word in each sentence.

What Do They Say?

DIRECTIONS Read the story. Add quotation marks to show what the characters say.

"Can I play soccer with you?" Consuela asked.

Anthony shook his head. We already have enough players.

I am sorry.

Just then, Luis called from the field, What time is it?

It's five o'clock, Anthony called back.

Luis walked from the field and said, I have to go home.

Well, now you can play, Anthony said to Consuela. We need another player on the team.

Great! Consuela said, as she took her place on the field.

Let's play! said Anthony to the team.

> **Dialogue**
>
> **Dialogue** is what characters say to one another. Use quotation marks to show a speaker's exact words.
>
> Patty said, **"Let's play soccer after school."**
>
> **"Okay,"** said Hiroe. **"That sounds fun!"**

DIRECTIONS Look at the picture of Cho and Emily. Write what each girl says.

1. Cho says, _____

   _____

   _____

   _____

2. Emily says, _____

   _____

   _____

Test tomorrow on Chapter 7!

Small Kindnesses

DIRECTIONS Anahita likes to tell one of Aesop's fables. Read how she tells it. Then rewrite her story. Change the underlined verbs to the past tense.

Past Tense

A **past tense verb** tells about an action that happened earlier, or in the past. Regular past tense verbs end in **–ed**. Follow the spelling rules to form the past tense.

| watch + ed = watch**ed** | smile – e + ed = smil**ed** |
| hop + p + ed = hop**ped** | try – y + i + ed = **tried** |

The Ant and the Dove

One morning, a dove <u>starts</u> to fly over a river. She <u>spies</u> an ant in the water. It <u>begs</u> for help. The dove <u>carries</u> it to the shore.

The next day, the ant <u>stops</u> in the forest. A hunter <u>traps</u> the dove. The ant <u>chomps</u> on the hunter's foot. The hunter <u>cries</u> out. The dove <u>escapes</u>.

The dove <u>smiles</u>. "Thank you, little ant!"

"Well, you <u>pull</u> me from the river," the ant <u>replies</u>, "so I <u>owe</u> you a favor!"

One morning, a dove started to fly over a river. _____

_____

_____

_____

_____

_____

_____

_____

_____

Tell It Again!

DIRECTIONS Retell a story with a partner.

1 **Study your storyboards. Answer the questions.**

- What story will you retell? _____

- What character will you be? _____

- What character will your partner be?

  _____

- What will your character say?

  _____

  _____

  _____

- What will your partner's character say?

  _____

  _____

  _____

  _____

2 **Practice retelling the story. Then retell it to another set of partners.**

3 **Ask your listeners what they think about your retelling.
Ask these questions.**

- Did we retell the events in order?   • Did we tell about all the events?

- Did we use order words?   • Did we use dialogue?

Use Your Talents!

DIRECTIONS Complete the paragraphs. Use present tense verbs in the first paragraph. Use past tense verbs in the second paragraph.

Monkey always _____enjoys_____ parties. He usually
               1. enjoy

_____ Meercat to go along. They _____ to see
   2. invite   **3. like**

their friends. They _____ all night. Meercat _____
               4. dance   **5. twirl**

better than any other dancer in the desert.

Last week, Monkey and Meercat _____attended_____ a party at Camel's house.
                      6. attend

Camel _____ to dance with Meercat. He _____ to keep
      7. ask   **8. try**

up with her. Finally, he _____ his silliness. Then he _____
              9. stop   **10. serve**

his famous pecan pie!

> ## Action Verbs
> An **action verb** tells what the subject does. The **tense** shows when the action happens.
>
> **Present Tense**
> The lion **roars**.
> The mouse **scurries**.
>
> **Past Tense**
> The lion **roared**.
> The mouse **scurried**.

DIRECTIONS Read the paragraph. Underline each present tense verb. Then rewrite the paragraph. Change the present tense verbs to past tense verbs.

> ## Aesop the Storyteller
> Aesop <u>lives</u> in Greece. He serves others as a slave. He watches people's actions. He uses animals as characters in stories. Many people stop to listen to his stories. Later, his master decides to free Aesop.

<u>Aesop lived</u> in Greece. _____

_____

_____

_____

© Hampton-Brown

CONTENT AREA CONNECTIONS

Study Aesop and His World

DIRECTIONS Work with a group. Follow the steps to make
a map of ancient Greece or to write a biography of Aesop.

☐ We will make a **map** of ancient Greece.

☐ We will write a **biography** of Aesop's life.

 Steps

 Steps

❶ Find information. List your sources.

☐ atlas _____

_____

☐ encyclopedia _____

_____

☐ Web site _____

_____

☐ other _____

**❷ Take notes. Write names of places you
will show on your map.**

• bordering countries _____

_____

_____

• important cities _____

_____

_____

• bodies of water _____

_____

❸ Present your information to the class.
• show your map
• tell about the countries and
  bodies of water near Greece
• point to important cities

❶ Find information. List your sources.

☐ encyclopedia _____

_____

☐ book _____

_____

☐ Web site _____

_____

☐ other _____

**❷ Take notes. Write information you will
tell about Aesop.**

• when Aesop lived _____

_____

• what Aesop's life was like _____

_____

• his most important works _____

_____

❸ Present your information to the class.
• read the biography aloud
• show pictures or dress up like Aesop

Friends Every Day

DIRECTIONS Complete the chart. Write two things you and a friend do every day.

	Time of Day	Activity
1.	morning	
2.	afternoon	
3.	night	

> ### Present Tense
> A **present tense verb** can tell about an action that happens over and over again.
>
> Leana **jogs** every day.
> On Sundays, I **visit** Grandpa.

DIRECTIONS Choose activities from the chart above. Write sentences to tell what you do every day.

4. _____

_____

5. _____

_____

6. _____

_____

7. _____

_____

8. _____

© Hampton-Brown

Express Yourself!

DIRECTIONS Write a poem. Tell about the perfect friend.
Finish each line with an infinitive.

> ### Infinitives
> An **infinitive** is a verb form. It starts with the word **to**.
> > I like **to chat**.
> > I have **to call** Ving.
>
> An infinitive can follow other verbs such as *want*, *like*, *need* and *have*.

The Perfect Friend

A perfect friend likes ___to spend time with me___ .

A perfect friend wants ___to explore things with me___ .

A perfect friend loves ___to let ME be ME___ !

This is the kind of friend I want to have:

When I ask for help, my friend is there _____ .

When I need to talk, my friend is there _____ .

When I am sad, my friend is there _____ .

This is the kind of friend I want to be:

When a friend asks for help, I am there _____ .

When a friend needs to talk, I am there _____ .

When a friend feels sad, I am there _____ .

A perfect friend likes _____ .

A perfect friend wants _____ .

A perfect friend loves _____ !

MORE ABOUT INFINITIVES Read your poem aloud to the class. Then make a class list.
Use verbs and infinitives to describe what a perfect friend is like.

Words About Friends

Use New Words in Context

DIRECTIONS Read each sentence. Replace the words in bold with new words. Write the new sentence. Read your sentences to a partner.

New Words

best friend

crazy about

every chance we got

go out of my way

go over

had our lives all planned out

stop to worry

talk and talk

that was all there was to it

1. Alfredo is my **favorite person**.

   <u>Alfredo is my best friend.</u>
   _____

2. I **do everything I can** to spend time with Alfredo. _____
   _____

3. We often **travel** to the dock to fish. _____
   _____

4. Both of us are **excited about** fishing. _____
   _____

5. On the dock, we **talk for a long time**. _____
   _____

6. Last summer, we went fishing **all the time**. _____
   _____

7. We didn't **take time to think** about anything else. _____
   _____

8. We would be fishermen for the rest of our lives—**we were sure of it**!

   We **knew what we wanted to do in the future**. _____
   _____
   _____

MORE ABOUT NEW WORDS Write sentences about your best friend.
Use the new words.

GRAMMAR: IRREGULAR PAST TENSE

What Was Parmele Like?

DIRECTIONS Read each sentence. Choose the correct verb.

> **Irregular Past Tense**
>
> The verbs **was** and **were** are past tense forms of the verb **be**. They tell about the past.
>
> > Lillie **was** my friend.
> > We **were** close.
>
> Use **was** to tell about one person or thing. Use **were** to tell about more than one person or thing.

1. Lessie Jones Little _____(was)/ were_____ born in Parmele, North Carolina.

2. Parmele _____was / were_____ very different in 1906.

3. Many African Americans _____was / were_____ low-paid farmers then.

4. They _____was / were_____ paid 50 cents a day.

5. One school _____was / were_____ for white children.

6. Two schools _____was / were_____ for African American children.

DIRECTIONS Write *was* or *were* to complete the paragraph.

   In 1906, Parmele _____was_____ a train town. Some
                          7.

men _____ workers for the railroad. Trains
        8.

_____ coming and going all day. Some
   9.

trains _____ for passengers. Other trains
          10.

_____ for freight, like food or animals. The train
   11.

station _____ a busy place. It _____ a gathering place.
            12.   **13.**

People _____ happy to spend time there.
           14.

MORE ABOUT THE IRREGULAR PAST TENSE Ask an adult, "What was our town like long ago?" Write a paragraph about the old days. Use the verbs *was* and *were*.

In a Time and Place

Setting
The **setting** is the place and the time a story happens. It answers the questions *Where?* and *When?*

DIRECTIONS Look at the words and photos in "My Best Friend." Write any clues that tell about the story's setting.

Page	Words	Photos
143	Lessie Jones Little was born in Parmele, North Carolina in 1906.	Their clothes are old-fashioned.
144		
145		
146		
147		

DIRECTIONS Write a paragraph to tell about the setting of "My Best Friend."

"My Best Friend" takes place _____

_____

_____

_____

_____

Relate Main Ideas and Details

DIRECTIONS Read the story. Add details from the story to finish
the tree diagram.

Best Buddies

Felix and Rosario are best friends. They
work together in math. After school, they play
softball. Sometimes Rosario goes to Felix's
house. They do their homework. Then they like
to watch the basketball game on television.

Main Idea   Details

Felix and Rosario
are best friends.

DIRECTIONS Write a paragraph about Felix and Rosario.
Use the ideas in your tree diagram.

Tell the main idea in
your **topic sentence**.

_____

_____

Give **details** to tell
more about the
main idea.

_____

_____

_____

Sum up your
paragraph. Write a
concluding sentence.

_____

_____

People Are Special

DIRECTIONS Follow the steps to write about people. Tell about your friends today and people from your past.

> ### Linking Verbs
> A **linking verb** connects the subject of a sentence to a word in the predicate.
>
> The word in the predicate can describe the subject.
>
> Ami **is** friendly.
>
> Or, the word can name the subject again.
>
> Anna and Boris **were** my grandparents.

1 Complete the lists.

	Names of People	Relationship	Words That Describe
1.	Samuel	classmate	helpful
2.			
3.			
4.			
5.			

2 Write two sentences about the present. Tell about one person in one sentence. Tell about two people in the other. Use linking verbs.

Linking Verbs

Present			Past	
am	is	are	was	were

6. Samuel is my classmate. _____

7. _____

8. _____

3 Write two sentences about the past. Tell about one person in one sentence. Tell about two people in the other. Use linking verbs.

9. _____

10. _____

Use a Chart

Charts

Charts present information in rows and columns. Read across rows and down columns in a chart.

DIRECTIONS Read the chart. Then answer the questions.

The **title** tells what the chart is about.

Students in Group 5

Name	Where They Were Born	Where They Live Now
Giana	Rome, Italy	Seaside, California
Oscar	Oaxaca, Mexico	Monterey, California
Nursal	Istanbul, Turkey	Monterey, California

The **headings** show types of information.

The **columns** go from top to bottom.

The **rows** go from left to right.

1. What is the title of the chart? Students in Group 5 _____

2. How many headings are in the chart? _____

3. How many rows are in the chart? _____

4. How many columns are in the chart? _____

5. What information is under the heading *Name*? _____

6. What does the chart compare? _____

   _____

7. In which row can you find information about Giana? _____

8. Where was Oscar born? _____

9. Where does Giana live now? _____

10. Compare the information about Giana and Nursal. What can you say about where

    they live now? _____

11. How are Oscar and Nursal the same? _____

12. What can you say about where all the people in the chart were born? _____

    _____

MORE ABOUT CHARTS Interview your group or class. Ask where they were born and where they live now. Make a chart.

Compare Generations

DIRECTIONS Interview an older person and a friend. Follow the steps.

1 **Choose whom you will interview. Write their names.**

I will interview _____ about life in the past.

I will interview _____ about life today.

2 **Prepare for the interview. Make a check in the box after you complete each step.**

☐ Call or visit each person. Arrange a time to talk or meet.

☐ Make a list of questions to ask. During the interview, you may think of more questions.

☐ Practice your interview with a partner.

3 **Conduct each interview. Ask your questions. Write the answers. Be sure to thank the person.**

4 **Look over your questions and answers. Organize the information. Use the chart.**

Subjects	Name: _____ Then (19 _ _)	Name: _____ Now (20 _ _)

5 **Study your chart. Compare what life was like in the past to how life is now. Share what you learned with the class.**

Example:

In the past, people waited for letters from their friends.

Today, people don't have to wait for letters. They can e-mail their friends.

Tell Family Stories

DIRECTIONS Read each sentence. Choose the correct verb.

Past Tense
A **past tense verb** tells what happened earlier, or in the past.
Use **was** to tell about one person, place, or thing.
Grandma **was** an immigrant. She **was** born in Romania.
Use **were** to tell about more than one person, place, or thing.
My grandparents **were** creative. They **were** musicians.

1. Melita's parents ___was /(were)___ from Romania.

2. Her father ___was / were___ from Bucharest.

3. He and his brother ___was / were___ doctors.

4. Melita's mother ___was / were___ from Constanta.

5. She ___was / were___ an art teacher.

6. When Melita ___was / were___ twelve, her family moved to Ohio.

7. Their new house ___was / were___ in the city of Columbus.

8. Her parents ___was / were___ happy to have a new start.

DIRECTIONS Write about your family history. Use the verbs *was* and *were*. Tell where people lived. Tell what they did. Add a map or a picture to show something about your family.

My Family Story

_____

_____

_____

_____

_____

_____

_____

_____

_____

Words That Go Together

New Words

advise
ancestor
dedicate
education
leader
pioneer
source of
support

Relate Words

DIRECTIONS Write each new word in the center of a box. What does the new word mean to you? Write your ideas in the corners of the box.

how to paint	read
education	
school	learn to cook

Three American Pioneers

Irregular Past Tense

Was and **were** are the past tense forms of the verb **be**.

Use **was** to tell about one person, place, or thing.
    Cornelius **was** a pilot.

Use **were** to tell about more than one person, place, or thing.
    The men **were** pioneers.

DIRECTIONS Read each sentence. Choose the correct verb.

1. Fredrick Douglass and Sojourner Truth ___was /(were)___ pioneers.

2. They ___was / were___ leaders in the 1800s.

3. They ___was / were___ against slavery.

4. Fredrick Douglass ___was / were___ an escaped slave.

5. His newspapers ___was / were___ famous all over the world.

6. Sojourner Truth ___was / were___ a slave, too.

7. Her speeches ___was / were___ very popular.

8. Both leaders ___was / were___ strong voices against slavery.

DIRECTIONS Read the article. Write *was* or *were* to complete each sentence.

Lewis Latimer, Inventor

Lewis Latimer ___was___ from Chelsea, Massachusetts.
        9.

Latimer _____ a soldier in the Civil War. Later, he
        10.

_____ a worker at a law firm. Latimer _____ good
    11.   12.

at drawing. His drawings _____ very detailed.
                            13.

Latimer _____ an inventor. He _____ a part of
        14.   15.

Thomas Edison's team. The men on the team _____ called
                                              16.

"Edison's Pioneers." They _____ impressed by Latimer's
                            17.

work with the light bulb. His inventions and writings _____
                                                        18.

very important.

Lewis Latimer's invention made electric light bulbs practical.

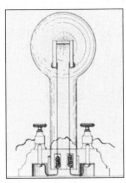

Latimer's light bulb

A Painter's Tribute

DIRECTIONS Read the paragraph. Underline each linking verb.

Washington, D.C., <u>is</u> Helen Zughaib's home. Helen's paintings look lively and colorful. The geometric shapes are bright. Sometimes, her subjects appear realistic. Sometimes, they seem imaginary. Helen is very talented. Her family must feel proud of her work.

Helen's family is Lebanese. Her grandmother was Syrian and Lebanese. She was an educated woman. She seemed very kind and patient. Helen's work is a tribute to her grandmother.

> **Linking Verbs**
>
> A **linking verb** connects the subject of the sentence to a word in the predicate.
>
> The word in the predicate can describe the subject.
>
> Your art **looks** creative.
>
> Or, the word can name the subject again.
>
> You **are** an artist.

DIRECTIONS Look at the painting by Helen Zughaib. Then complete each sentence. Use words from the box.

is the artist	is a painting
looks busy	are ferns
is the Lincoln Memorial	appear tall
look colorful	seems thick

This is Helen Zughaib's painting of the Lincoln Memorial. The original painting is very colorful.

1. The picture on this page

   <u>is a painting</u> _____ .

2. Helen Zughaib _____ .

3. The building _____ .

4. The painting _____ .

5. The feathery plants _____ .

6. The columns _____ .

7. The patterns _____ .

8. The roof _____ .

© Hampton-Brown

The Art of Enrique Chagoya

DIRECTIONS Read each sentence. Underline the past tense verb. Write *regular* or *irregular*. Look on Handbook pages 422 and 424–425 if you need help.

> **Irregular Past Tense**
>
> Regular past tense verbs end in **–ed**. **Irregular past tense verbs** do not end in **–ed**. They have special forms to show the past tense.
>
>   Yesterday, Emily **drew** a picture of her uncle.

1. The artist <u>decided</u> to paint a portrait.   _____regular_____

2. First, he studied a photograph of his parents.   _____

3. Then, he drew a sketch in pencil.   _____

4. Next, he began to add paint.   _____

5. He spent many hours on the portrait.   _____

6. He wanted it to look just right.   _____

DIRECTIONS Complete the passage. Use verbs from the box.

Irregular Past Tense Verbs			
became	gave	told	taught
came	went	won	was

Enrique Chagoya grew up in Mexico. His father taught him how to draw.

Enrique Chagoya grew up in Mexico. His nurse _____told_____ him
                                                    7.

stories about his culture. His father _____ him drawing lessons.
                                              8.

His mother _____ a source of love and support. Enrique
                  9.

_____ to college in Mexico City. In the late 1970s, Enrique and his
    10.

wife _____ to the United States. His work _____ awards.
        11.   **12.**

He _____ a professor. Enrique's ancestors _____ him
      13.   **14.**

many lessons. Now he teaches the lessons to his students.

Identify Cause and Effect

DIRECTIONS Read the story. Then complete each sentence.
Write the missing cause or effect. Use *because* or *so*.

> ### Cause and Effect
> An **effect** is something that happens. A **cause** is the reason it happens.
>
> • Use *because* before a cause.
>
>   I paint pictures **because** I love art.
>
> • Use *so* before an effect.
>
>   I love art **so** I paint pictures.

A Labor of Love

Ying Lak goes to art class on Saturdays. This Saturday, the teacher asks the class to make a drawing to honor someone.

Ying Lak thinks for a long time. She decides to draw a picture to honor her parents.

First, she draws her parents' faces. Then she thinks about what they like to do. Her mother loves to garden. Her father works at the library. She decides to put flowers and books in her drawing. Red and green are lucky colors. She adds a red and green border.

After class, Ying Lak shows the drawing to her parents. She wants them to see her work. They love the drawing! They are happy Ying cares about them.

---

1. Ying Lak decides to draw a picture <u>because she wants to honor her parents</u> .

2. Her mother loves to garden _____ .

3. Her father works at the library _____ .

4. Red and green are lucky colors _____ .

5. Ying shows the drawing to her parents _____ .

6. Ying's parents love the drawing _____ .

DIRECTIONS Paraphrase the story. Write it in your own words. Show causes and effects.

_____

_____

_____

_____

_____

_____

_____

_____

Give Me a Clue

DIRECTIONS Read the passage. Look at the underlined words. Complete the chart.

My father was born in Northern China. When he was young, his family emigrated. They moved from China to the country of Vietnam. Vietnam was a fascinating place. There were many exciting things to see and do.

After high school, my father moved to Taiwan. He went to a university. He studied and learned from many teachers at the school. A friend introduced a new girl there. He said her name was Hingling. In a few years, Hingling and my father finished all their studies and graduated. Then they got married and had me!

Context Clues

When you see a new word, read the other words around it. They can give **context clues**, or hints, to help you find the word's meaning.

I honor my grandparents and other **ancestors.**

Context clue: *my grandparents*
Meaning: family members who lived before me

New Word	Context Clues	Meaning
emigrated	moved, from China, to Vietnam	went to live in another country
fascinating		
university		
introduced		
graduated		

CONTENT AREA CONNECTIONS

Research an Ancestor's Country

DIRECTIONS Compare an ancestor's life with your life in the United States.
Follow the steps.

1 **Make a plan.**

• My ancestor's country: _____

• Topics about the country to research: ☐ traditions   ☐ climate   ☐ other _____

2 **Find information about the country. Write the names of your sources.**

☐ encyclopedia   ☐ interview   ☐ Web site   ☐ book

_____   _____   _____   _____

_____   _____   _____   _____

3 **Take notes in a Venn diagram.**

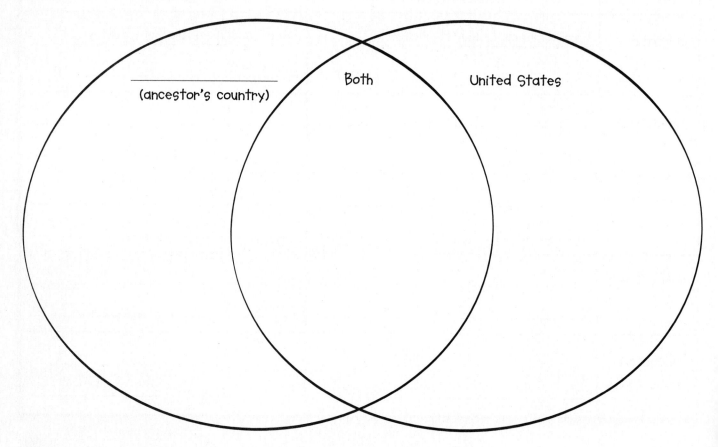

_____
(ancestor's country)   Both   United States

4 **Share your information with the class. Tell how life in your
ancestor's country is the same as your life in the United States.
Tell how it is different.**

BUILD LANGUAGE AND VOCABULARY

Explaining Family Traits

DIRECTIONS Read each sentence. Underline the verb.
Then write *present tense* or *past tense*.

1. Last week, I <u>went</u> to my grandpa's house.   _____past tense_____

2. He shared stories about his childhood.   _____

3. Grandpa always shows us old photographs.   _____

4. I found an old picture of my father.   _____

5. He was skinny and tall.   _____

6. I look just like my father!   _____

DIRECTIONS Complete the sentences. Use the past tense form of the
underlined verb.

Nana Henka

Sabina

7. Sabina <u>is</u> my little sister. She _____was_____ five last year.

8. Sabina <u>looks</u> different every year. At first, she _____ like my
   great-great-grandmother.

9. My sister <u>has</u> dark brown hair. Nana Henka _____ dark brown hair, too.

10. Her eyes <u>are</u> green. Nana Henka's eyes _____ dark green.

11. Sabina <u>smiles</u> like my great-great-grandmother. Nana Henka _____
    a lot.

12. Sabina <u>sings</u> to herself all the time. Nana Henka _____ on stage
    all her life.

It's All in the Family!

New Words

- combination
- family resemblance
- gene
- genetics
- identical twins
- inherit
- relative
- trait

Use New Words in Context

DIRECTIONS Read each sentence. Write *T* for true. Write *F* for false.

___T___ **1.** You can **inherit** a **trait** from a **relative**.

_____ **2.** You can share a **family resemblance** with a friend.

_____ **3.** **Identical twins** have the same **combination** of genes.

_____ **4.** Scientists who study **genetics** learn about parts of a **gene**.

Use New Words in Context

DIRECTIONS Read each sentence. Add the correct new word.

5. Brown eyes are a _____ trait _____ of mine.

6. I look like my Aunt Sue. There is a _____ .

7. My father learns about cell parts that pass from parent to child.

   He studies the science of _____ .

8. My two brothers have the exact same cell parts. They were born

   at the same time. They are _____ .

9. My cousin is the _____ I like the most

   in my family.

10. A _____ is a part of my cells that tells

   my body how to grow.

11. Everyone in my family has freckles. We _____

   them from my grandparents.

12. I have mother's curly hair and father's brown eyes. I have a mix, or

   _____ , of my father's and mother's genes.

GRAMMAR: DEMONSTRATIVE PRONOUNS

These Are Family Treasures

DIRECTIONS Look at the pictures. Answer the questions. Use *this*, *that*, *these*, and *those*.

> **Demonstrative Pronouns**
>
> A **demonstrative pronoun** points out a specific noun without naming it.
>
> > **This** is my grandfather.
> > Are **those** your relatives?
>
> Use **this** and **these** for things that are near.
> Use **that** and **those** for things that are far.

Natalia

Mikhail

1 **What does Natalia say about her treasures?**

1. " <u>These are family treasures.</u>
   _____ "

2. " _____
   _____ "

2 **What does Natalia tell Mikhail about his treasures?**

3. " <u>Those are cute nesting dolls.</u>
   _____ "

4. " _____
   _____ "

3 **What does Mikhail say about his treasures?**

5. " _____
   _____ "

6. " _____
   _____ "

4 **What does Mikhail tell Natalia about her treasures?**

7. " _____
   _____ "

8. " _____
   _____ "

MORE ABOUT DEMONSTRATIVE PRONOUNS What else are Natalia and Mikhail saying?
Write more sentences. Use a demonstrative pronoun in each sentence.

Reading Nonfiction

DIRECTIONS Follow the steps to read the nonfiction article.

1 **Look at the article before you read.**

1. What is the title? What are the headings?

Title: _____

Headings: _____

2. What does the picture show? _____

_____

_____

3. What will the article be about?

_____

_____

2 **Write your questions about the topic.**

_____

_____

_____

_____

3 **Now read the article. Take notes.**

_____

_____

_____

_____

_____

_____

_____

_____

4 **Share what you learned with the class.**

The Parts of a Cell

Pairs of Chromosomes Every living creature is made of cells. Most cells have 23 pairs of chromosomes. That is a total of 46 chromosomes in each cell. You get half your chromosomes from your mother. The other half comes from your father.

Different Genes Chromosomes hold genes that tell your body how to grow. The genes say whether you will be tall, short, dark, or light. Some traits come from one gene. Other traits come from gene combinations. There are many possible combinations. That is why there will never be another person just like you!

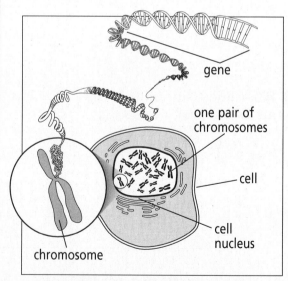

gene

one pair of chromosomes

cell

cell nucleus

chromosome

The human cell has chromosomes and genes that tell your body how to grow.

GRAMMAR: NEGATIVE SENTENCES

Don't ~~Never~~ Do That!
Ever

(handwritten: "Ever" inserted above, caret mark below)

DIRECTIONS Read each pair of sentences. Underline the correct sentence.

> **Negative Sentences**
> Use a **negative word** to make a sentence mean "no."
>   Ana's mom wears glasses.
>   Ana's mom **never** wears glasses.
> Use only one negative word in a sentence.

1. Lim never learned nothing about genetics.
   <u>Lim never learned anything about genetics.</u>

2. There were no books nowhere in the library about it.
   There were no books anywhere in the library about it.

3. He did not share any of the family resemblances.
   He did not share none of the family resemblances.

4. He did not look like anyone in his family.
   He did not look like no one in his family.

5. He never saw none of his resemblance to his grandfather.
   He never saw his resemblance to his grandfather.

DIRECTIONS Read each sentence. Write it as a negative sentence. Use the word in parentheses.

6. Some people look like their relatives. (**not**)

   Some people do not look like their relatives.

7. People inherit traits from their teachers. (**nobody**)

   _____

8. My cousin looks something like me. (**nothing**)

   _____

9. Cousins always have the exact same genetic information. (**never**)

   _____

10. Everyone looks just like you. (**no one**)

   _____

CONTENT AREA CONNECTIONS

Study Genetics

DIRECTIONS Answer the questions to complete the Punnett square.

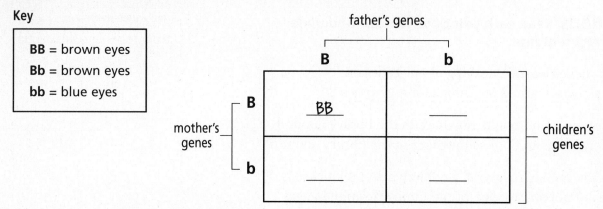

Key

BB = brown eyes
Bb = brown eyes
bb = blue eyes

1. What is the father's gene in column 1? __B__ What is the mother's gene in row 1? __B__

   Combine the genes. Write the combination in the Punnett square.

2. What is the father's gene in column 2? ____ What is the mother's gene in row 1? ____

   Combine the genes. Write the combination in the Punnett square. Put the capital
   letter first.

3. What is the father's gene in column 1? ____ What is the mother's gene in row 2? ____

   Combine the genes. Write the combination in the Punnett square. Put the capital
   letter first.

4. What is the father's gene in column 2? ____ What is the mother's gene in row 2? ____

   Combine the genes. Write the combination in the Punnett square.

_____

DIRECTIONS Answer the questions about the Punnett square.

5. Study the key. Both parents have the genes **Bb** for eye color.

   What color eyes do they have? _____

6. How many squares show children with brown eyes? _____

7. How many squares show children with blue eyes? _____

8. If the parents have only one child, what color will her eyes most likely be? _____

© Hampton-Brown

UNIT 4 MIND MAP

Community

DIRECTIONS Think about the communities you belong to. Write the name of each group on the mind map. Then read each selection in this unit. Add to the map ideas you learn about communities.

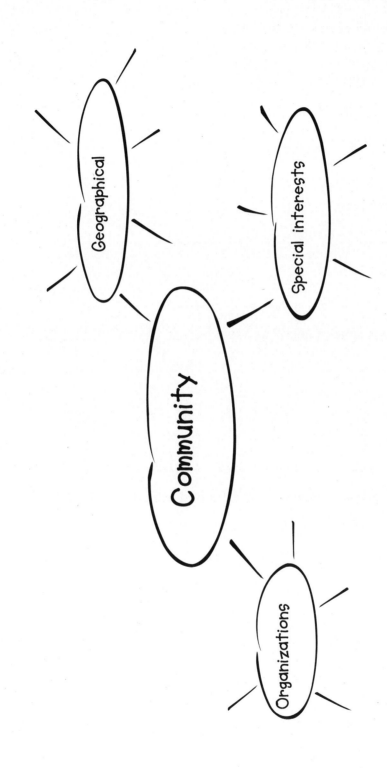

A Better Future

DIRECTIONS Tell what will happen. Use future tense verbs to complete each sentence.

> **Future Tense**
> A **future tense verb** tells about an action that will happen later. To show the future tense, use the helping verb **will** with a main verb.
>   We **will learn** about pollution.
> In a question, the subject comes between the helping verb and the main verb.
>   **Will** we **help** the Earth?

1. If people leave trash everywhere, _____

   _our community will look awful_____ .

   If people pick up trash, _____

   _____ .

2. If people drive everywhere, _____

   _____ .

   If drivers carpool, _____

   _____ .

3. If people throw plastic, paper, and cans away, _____

   _____ .

   If every family recycles, _____

   _____ .

DIRECTIONS Rewrite each sentence. Change the underlined verb to the future tense.

4. Our class <u>sponsors</u> a community clean-up in March.

   _Our class will sponsor a community clean-up in March._____

5. We <u>collect</u> trash at the beach.

   _____

6. Mr. Leung <u>drives</u> us to the recycling center.

   _____

7. <u>Do</u> we <u>separate</u> glass and paper?

   _____

8. <u>Do</u> we <u>earn</u> money for recycling?

   _____

Something in Common

Relate Words

DIRECTIONS Sort the new words into groups. Label each group. You may write some new words more than once. Add more words you know.

New Words

- benefit
- common
- common ground
- commons
- forest
- fossil fuel
- natural resource
- sustain
- village
- villager

Places to Live

village
forest
_____
_____
_____

Words That Look Alike

village
villager
_____
_____
_____

Natural Resources

forest
water
_____
_____
_____

_____

_____
_____
_____
_____

_____

_____
_____
_____
_____

_____

_____
_____
_____
_____

GRAMMAR: THERE IS/ARE; THERE WAS/WERE

There Are Always Solutions!

There Is/Are; There Was/Were

Some sentences begin with **There is, There are, There was,** or **There were.** In these sentences, the <u>subject</u> comes after the verb.

There is a <u>problem</u>.
There were too many <u>sheep</u>.

Use the chart to choose the correct verb.

	One	**More Than One**
In the present	is	are
In the past	was	were

DIRECTIONS Circle the correct verb to complete each sentence.

1. There _____**is /(was)**_____ a village long ago.

2. There _____**was / were**_____ too many sheep on the commons.

3. There _____**was / were**_____ a solution to the problem.

4. There _____**is / are**_____ always a way to share space.

5. There _____**is / are**_____ usually many choices.

DIRECTIONS Work with a partner. Write *is*, *are*, *was*, or *were* to complete the sentences.

Kim and Saba were good neighbors. Then one day, Saba's dog dug up Kim's

garden. There _____ flowers all over the place!
　　　　　　　　　6.

So Saba built a fence. Soon Kim knocked at Saba's door. "There _____
　　　　　　　　　　　　　　　　　　　　　　　　　　　　　　　　　7.

a problem," Kim said. "Your fence is on my land. There _____ papers
　　　　　　　　　　　　　　　　　　　　　　　　　　　　　　8.

to prove it." There _____ only one thing to do. Saba took down the fence.
　　　　　　　　　　　9.

The next day, Kim showed Saba more dead flowers.

"I know," Saba groaned. "There _____ a problem."
　　　　　　　　　　　　　　　　　　10.

Kim said, "There _____ always solutions. We can
　　　　　　　　　　　　11.

build a new fence on your side." So they built a new fence.

The next day, there _____ presents at Kim's door.
　　　　　　　　　　　　　12.

"Oh, wonderful!" he said. "I always wanted a dog!"

LITERARY ANALYSIS: THEME

A Universal Message

DIRECTIONS Follow the steps to find the theme of the folk tale.

Theme
The **theme** of a story is its message about life. Some themes can be found in stories from many cultures.

1 **Read the folk tale.**

How Coyote Helped Man

Long ago, there was no winter on Earth. All of the animals and Man were comfortable. Then one day, it began to grow cold. Coyote and the other animals had fur to keep them warm. Man did not. Coyote worried about Man.

Coyote wanted to help Man. He knew that Fire Beings lived far up in the mountains. They guarded a piece of the sun. Coyote thought that if Man had a piece of the sun, he could stay warm all winter.

Coyote went up the mountain to the place where the Fire Beings lived. He took some of the fire.

Coyote brought the fire to Man. Man stayed warm all winter. Man thanked Coyote for his gift. Man is no longer cold in winter because of Coyote's help.

2 **Think about what happened in the story. Answer the questions.**

1. How did Coyote feel about Man? _____

_____

2. What did Coyote do to help Man? _____

_____

3. How did Man feel about Coyote's actions? _____

_____

4. What can we learn from Coyote's actions? _____

_____

3 **Write what you think the message of the folk tale is.**

The theme of the folk tale is: _____

_____ .

Save the Earth!

How to Play: Save the Earth!

1. Play in a group of three. One person is "the judge." The other two are players.

2. Recycle a small object as a game piece.

3. If you are players, stop at each space. Take turns using the word to ask and answer questions. Use the future tense. For example:
   Player 1: How **will** you **save** paper?
   Player 2: I **will recycle** it.
   Player 2: How **will** you **protect** the ocean?
   Player 1: I **will keep** waste out of storm drains.

4. If you are the judge, listen for the future tense. Send the players back one space for a wrong answer.

5. When both players reach THE FUTURE!, they have SAVED THE EARTH!

The Future

START

paper

ocean

glass

air

plastic

rivers

gas

fish

aluminum

forests

Earth-Friendly Books

DIRECTIONS Find out more about the author of "Common Ground."
Use a K-W-L chart. Follow the steps.

1 Write what you know about Molly Bang.

2 Then write what you want to know.

K What I Know	W What I Want to Know	L What I Learned
	What other books has she written about the environment?	

3 Read about Molly Bang. Add what you learned to the K-W-L chart.

Molly Bang: Earth-Friendly Author

Molly Bang writes and illustrates books. She was born in 1943 in Princeton, New Jersey. She enjoys telling fables and stories from many different cultures. Her books are often funny and sometimes mysterious. She uses many different materials to create her illustrations. She may use watercolor, paper, cloth, yarn, or clay—or maybe all of these materials together.

Molly wrote other books, like *Common Ground*, that are about the environment. In 1996, she wrote a book called *Chattanooga Sludge*. It is about a man who worked to clean a creek in Tennessee. Molly illustrated the book with old magazines to show the importance of recycling.

Molly Bang has won many awards for her books and illustrations, including the Caldecott Honor Book Award and the Giverney Award.

Molly Bang is a successful author.

GRAMMAR: ADJECTIVES THAT COMPARE

The Most Beautiful Place!

DIRECTIONS Write the correct form of the adjective in parentheses. See Handbook page 419 for help.

1. Forests are _____ more peaceful _____ than towns. (**peaceful**)

2. Rain forests are the _____ forests of all. (**lush**)

3. The _____ rain forest in the world is near my old home in Costa Rica. (**pretty**)

4. The trees here are _____ than trees in Costa Rica. (**short**)

5. Costa Rica has the _____ forests in the whole world! (**wonderful**)

Adjectives That Compare

To compare two things, add **–er** to short adjectives. For long adjectives, use the word **more**. Also use **than**.

> My sheep are **hungrier than** yours.
> Your sheep are **more attractive than** mine.

To compare three or more things, add **–est** to short adjectives. Use the word **most** for long adjectives.

> Esin's sheep are the **hungriest** of all.
> Hilmi's sheep are the **most attractive** sheep on the commons.

DIRECTIONS Label the pictures. Use the correct form of the adjective. Then write a sentence.

6. _____ cloudy _____ _____ _____

7. _____ crowded _____ _____ _____

8. Write a sentence about some of the pictures. Use an adjective that compares.

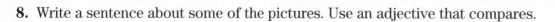

_____

_____

Using an Encyclopedia

DIRECTIONS Study the encyclopedia article. Then answer the questions.

Encyclopedia

An **encyclopedia** has information about many topics. Topics are listed in alphabetical order. You can use print, electronic, or on-line encyclopedias.

Pollution 253

The **entry word** is the **title** of the article.

A **heading** tells what the section is about.

A **subheading** tells what the paragraph is about.

POLLUTION

Pollution hurts the environment. It makes the air, land, and water dirty or dangerous.

Air Pollution

The Causes of Air Pollution Many things pollute the air. Some pollutants come from natural causes like volcanoes, fires, and dust. Most air pollution comes from cars, factories, and waste.

The Effects of Air Pollution Dirty air can make humans and animals sick. Sometimes the pollutants create **acid rain**. Dangerous chemicals fall to the earth and water below. Air pollution traps energy around the Earth and adds to the **greenhouse effect**. This causes **global warming**.

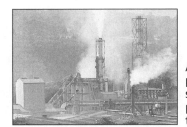

A factory produces smoke and pollutes the air.

Some Solutions for Air Pollution There are many ways to cut down air pollution. People can **carpool**. They can stop burning trash. Factories can put fewer chemicals into the air.

Land Pollution

The Causes of Land Pollution Many things cause land pollution. When people do not throw trash away correctly, they create litter. **Chemicals** from farming can soak into the earth.

Pictures and **captions** give more information.

Key words and **details** often appear in dark print.

1. What is the main topic of the article? Circle it. Underline the headings and subheadings.

2. What ideas does the article tell about? _____

_____

3. What are some key words that tell about the effects of air pollution? _____

_____

4. What do the picture and the caption tell about the topic? _____

_____

5. You want to learn how to stop air pollution. Where in the article would you look? _____

_____

Study Environmental Problems

DIRECTIONS Work with a group. Follow the steps to research an environmental problem.

1 Circle the problem your group will study.

Environmental Problems			
oil spills	water pollution	loss of forests	ozone layer
over-fishing	litter	loss of fossil fuels	air pollution
chemical dumping	toxic waste	acid rain	greenhouse effect

2 Where will you find information? Mark the sources you use. Write the titles.

☐ books ☐ magazines ☐ Web sites ☐ encyclopedias

_____ _____ _____ _____

_____ _____ _____ _____

3 Read about the problem and take notes.

4 Then organize your ideas. Use your notes to complete the chart. Brainstorm solutions with your group. Add them to the chart.

Environmental Problems and Solutions

Problems	Causes	Effects	Solutions

5 Share your information with the class. Show your chart, make a poster, or role-play a problem and its solution.

We Can Do It!

DIRECTIONS Which helping verb goes with the meaning?
Write it in the sentence.

> **Helping Verbs**
>
> Some verbs are made up of more than one word. A **helping verb** comes before the main verb.
>
> We **should** protect our resources.
> We **must** recycle cans.
> Everyone **can** help.
>
> | Helping Verb | Purpose |
> |---|---|
> | should | tells about a responsibility |
> | must | tells about a need |
> | can | tells about an ability |

1. **a need:**   We _____must_____ work harder to save our natural resources.

2. **an ability:**   We _____ buy recycled paper.

3. **a need:**   We _____ develop better public transportation.

4. **a responsibility:** We _____ not pollute our oceans.

5. **a need:**   We _____ stop wasting plastic.

6. **a responsibility:** People _____ carry their own bags to the store.

7. **an ability:**   I _____ reuse plastic water bottles.

8. **an ability:**   We _____ discover many ways to help.

DIRECTIONS Write sentences to tell people to protect our planet.
Use a different helping verb in each sentence. Choose one sentence
as a caption for a poster.

9. We should protect our forests. _____

10. _____

_____

11. _____

_____

12. _____

_____

We can pick up
trash at the
beach!

Words About Earth

New Words

- crystal clean
- earth/Earth
- life
- nation
- planet
- rain forest
- source of power
- stream
- up to me
- valley

Identify Definitions

DIRECTIONS Write each new word next to its definition.

1. a small river _____ stream

2. something I should do _____

3. ground; our planet _____

4. clear and pure _____

5. low ground between mountains _____

6. living things _____

7. a community of people of one country _____

8. object in space _____

9. something that gives energy _____

10. a place with lots of trees and rain _____

Relate Words

DIRECTIONS Underline the new words in the Table of Contents. Complete the sentences to tell what each chapter title means. Use your own words. Share your sentences with a partner.

The Planet Earth

Chapter	Title	Page
1.	The Stream and Valley: The Beauty of a Nation 8	
2.	Crystal Clean Rain: A Source of Power and Life 16	
3.	The Rain Forest: It's Up to Me to Help Save It 24	

Chapter 1 is about _____ .

Chapter 2 is about _____ .

Chapter 3 is about _____ .

© Hampton-Brown

GRAMMAR: HELPING VERBS (MODALS)

Many Sources of Power

wind power

solar power

water power

Helping Verbs

Some **helping verbs** tell about things that are possible. The helping verb comes before the main verb.

We **could** work together.
We **can** make a difference.

DIRECTIONS Work with a partner. Talk about the rules for helping verbs.

Helping Verb	What It Tells About	Example
can, could	an ability	We **can** work together.
could, may, might	a possibility	We **could** help the Earth.
must	a need	I **must** do what I can.
should	a responsibility	I **should** do my best.
will	an intent or plan	I **will** keep trying.
would	a wish or custom	We **would** make a big difference.

DIRECTIONS Complete each sentence with a helping verb. Use the meanings in the chart to choose the helping verb you want.

1. In the past, we _____would_____ only use energy from coal, oil, and gas.

2. These fuels _____ cause pollution.

3. Today, we _____ use other sources of energy.

4. We _____ use solar energy from the sun.

5. We _____ use energy from wind and water.

6. Scientists _____ learn more about energy all the time.

7. We _____ use up our resources someday.

8. New discoveries _____ help us save the planet.

MORE ABOUT HELPING VERBS Compare your sentences with a partner's sentences. Are the meanings of your sentences different? In what ways?

Wolves!

Wolves are very protective of their cubs.

Plural Nouns

You can form most plurals by adding –s to a singular noun. Other nouns follow special rules.

For nouns with a **consonant** plus **y**, change **y** to **i** and add –**es**: city → **cities**

For nouns with a **vowel** plus **y**, just add –**s**: day → **days**

For most nouns with an **f** or **fe**, change the **f** to **v** and add –**es**: leaf → **leaves**

Some nouns have irregular plural forms:
child → **children**
foot → **feet**

DIRECTIONS Rewrite each sentence. Change the singular nouns in parentheses into plural nouns. See Handbook pages 410–411 for help.

1. Many (creature) live their (life) on Earth.

   Many creatures live their lives on Earth.

2. (Wolf) share this beautiful planet with (person).

   _____

3. They have interesting (habit) and (way) of hunting.

   _____

4. They often attack bigger (animal), such as sick buffaloes and their (calf).

   _____

5. (Adult) feed their (cub) chewed meat.

   _____

6. Sometimes (rancher) think wolves are their (enemy).

   _____

7. When food (supply) are low, wolves hunt for animals in the farms and (valley).

   _____

8. (Man) and (woman) must discover how to share the planet with wolves.

   _____

Beneath the Sea

DIRECTIONS Write prepositions to finish the sentences.

Prepositions

Prepositions help to show time, location, direction, and other details.
The song comes **from** the ocean.
It traveled **across** the sea **to** my heart.

Some Prepositions

Time	Location	Direction	Other
during	below	from	of
on	off	around	with
after	near	through	among
in	in	into	by

1. A U.S. program protects sea water _____around_____ the world.

2. Fagatele Bay is a tiny marine sanctuary _____ the coast of American Samoa.

3. You can get there by boat _____ Pago Pago.

4. It was named a national marine sanctuary _____ April 29th, 1986.

5. The sanctuary is south _____ the equator.

6. It is 1000 miles _____ the equator.

7. Slopes _____ the bay contain rain forests.

8. The sanctuary protects a coral reef _____ the water.

9. Colorful fish swim _____ the coral beds.

10. Lobsters and crabs live _____ the bay, too.

11. They share the bay _____ parrot fish and sharks.

12. Whales and sea turtles visit the bay _____ parts of the year.

Lots of sea life lives in the bay.

Analyze Persuasive Techniques

DIRECTIONS Read "Protecting Our Planet" again. Add more of Raffi's words to the chart.
Then answer the question.

```
┌─────────────────────────────────────────────────────────┐
│              Persuasive Techniques                        │
└─────────────────────────────────────────────────────────┘
                          ↓
```

```
┌─────────────────────────────────────────────────────────┐
│          Words that make you love the Earth               │
│                                                           │
│  • big, beautiful planet        • _____     │
│  • source of power              • _____     │
│  • _____          • _____     │
│  • _____          • _____     │
└─────────────────────────────────────────────────────────┘
                          ↓
```

```
┌─────────────────────────────────────────────────────────┐
│            Words that make you feel sad                   │
│                                                           │
│  • rainforests are crying       • _____     │
│  • rain we used to know         • _____     │
│  • _____          • _____     │
│  • _____          • _____     │
└─────────────────────────────────────────────────────────┘
                          ↓
```

```
┌─────────────────────────────────────────────────────────┐
│              Words that ask for help                      │
│                                                           │
│  • help this planet Earth       • _____     │
│  • it's up to me, it's up to you  • _____     │
│  • _____          • _____     │
│  • _____          • _____     │
└─────────────────────────────────────────────────────────┘
```

Did Raffi persuade you to take care of the Earth? Tell a partner why or why not.

GRAMMAR: INDEFINITE PRONOUNS

Everyone Can Help

DIRECTIONS Finish the song. Use indefinite pronouns.

Some Indefinite Pronouns

Person		Place	Thing
anybody	anyone	anywhere	anything
somebody	everybody	somewhere	something
someone	everyone	everywhere	everything

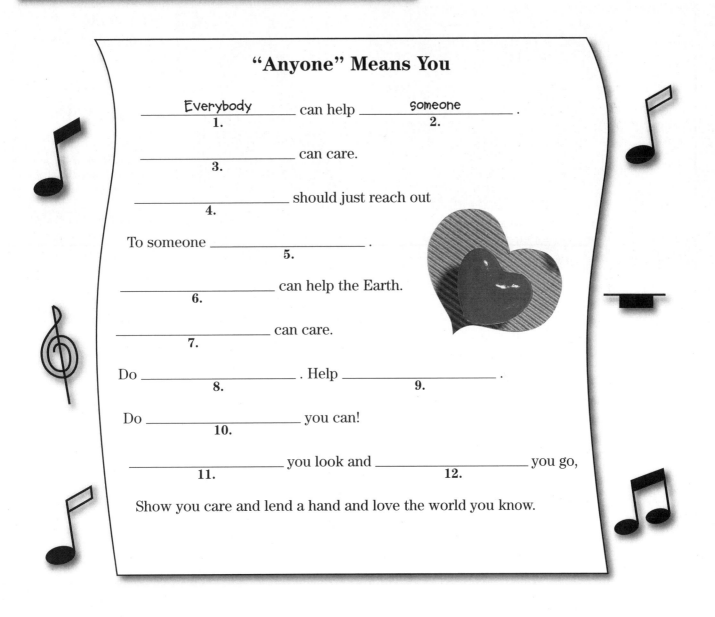

"Anyone" Means You

_____Everybody_____ can help _____someone_____ .
      1.   2.

_____ can care.
      3.

_____ should just reach out
      4.

To someone _____ .
            5.

_____ can help the Earth.
      6.

_____ can care.
      7.

Do _____ . Help _____ .
      8.   9.

Do _____ you can!
      10.

_____ you look and _____ you go,
      11.   12.

Show you care and lend a hand and love the world you know.

Learn About Propaganda

DIRECTIONS Work with a partner. Follow the steps to study propaganda.

1 Study the advertisements. Then decide what propaganda techniques are being used. Complete the chart.

Propaganda Techniques

Propaganda techniques try to make you feel or think a certain way. Advertisers use propaganda techniques to convince you to buy a product.

- A **glittering generality** uses words like *Better! New!* to say that a product is special.
- The **bandwagon technique** tells you to do something because other people are doing it.
- **Name calling** is saying bad things about another product.

Look at these kids. They're cool, confident, and happy. They wear *Cool Kid Jeans*. All the cool kids you know wear *Cool Kid Jeans*. Other jeans are just boring!

Buy *Cool Kid Jeans* today!

Are you tired of the same old bread?

Then it's time to try Earthy Bread.

Thank goodness for Earthy Bread. It's 100% new, 100% natural, and 100% delicious!

Earthy Bread
The bread that all healthy people eat.

	Propaganda Techniques		
Product	**Glittering Generality**	**Bandwagon Technique**	**Name Calling**
Cool Kid Jeans			
Earthy Bread			

2 Find more advertisements. Look in magazines and newspapers, or on the Internet. Listen to television commercials or the radio. Then complete the chart.

Product	Propaganda Techniques	Opinion
Product: _____ _____ Source: ☐ magazine ☐ newspaper ☐ television ☐ radio ☐ Internet	☐ glittering generality ☐ bandwagon ☐ name calling Examples: _____ _____ _____ _____	☐ The techniques worked. ☐ The techniques did not work. Why or why not: _____ _____ _____ _____
Product: _____ _____ Source: ☐ magazine ☐ newspaper ☐ television ☐ radio ☐ Internet	☐ glittering generality ☐ bandwagon ☐ name calling Examples: _____ _____ _____ _____	☐ The techniques worked. ☐ The techniques did not work. Why or why not: _____ _____ _____ _____
Product: _____ _____ Source: ☐ magazine ☐ newspaper ☐ television ☐ radio ☐ Internet	☐ glittering generality ☐ bandwagon ☐ name calling Examples: _____ _____ _____ _____	☐ The techniques worked. ☐ The techniques did not work. Why or why not: _____ _____ _____ _____

3 Choose an advertisement. Share it with the class. Use your chart to talk about the advertisement.

Use Audio-Visual Resources

Audio-Visual Resources
A **resource** is something that gives information. An **audio-visual resource** gives information using sounds, pictures, or moving images.

DIRECTIONS Work in a small group. Follow the steps to learn how to use audio-visual resources.

1 Tell how each audio-visual resource can add interest to a report. Complete the sentences.

audio cassettes and CDs

Audio cassettes and CDs let you _hear_
sounds such as speeches, animals sounds,
music, and habitats .

They also let you _record sounds and play_
them back .

photographs and drawings

Photographs show _____
_____
_____ .

Drawings can show _____
_____
_____ .

videos

Videos can show _____
_____
_____ .

Videos can also _____
_____
_____ .

maps

Maps can show _____
_____
_____ .

Interactive maps can _____
_____
_____ .

the Internet

The Internet can provide _____
_____
_____ .

It can also _____
_____

CD Roms

CD Roms _____
_____
_____ .

CD Roms can also _____
_____
_____ .

2 Choose an endangered species. Find information about your animal.
Look for resources with audio-visuals. Complete the chart.

Endangered Species: _____

Encyclopedia	Magazine or Book	The Internet
My source:	My source:	My source:
Audio-visual resources available from this source:	Audio-visual resources available from this source:	Audio-visual resources available from this source:

3 Plan how you can use each audio-visual resource in a presentation.

 vides

audio cassettes and CDs

_____

_____

_____

_____

maps

 photographs and drawings

_____

_____

_____

_____

4 Share an audio-visual resource with your class. Use it to briefly tell about your
endangered species.

Prepare for an Earthquake!

DIRECTIONS Read what to do in an earthquake. Tell someone else what to do. Write a command.

> **Commands**
>
> A **command** tells someone to do something.
>   Read that sign to me.
>
> The subject of the sentence is **you**. It is understood. It is not spoken.
>   **(You)** read that sign to me.

1. You can make a plan.

   Make a plan.

   _____

2. People should keep a flashlight and a radio in the house.

   _____

3. It is good to keep bottled water in your home.

   _____

4. You can stand in a doorway or get under a table during a quake.

   _____

5. You should watch out for falling objects.

   _____

6. People need to stay away from windows.

   _____

7. You should not wander away from your friends or family.

   _____

   _____

8. People should try to stay calm.

   _____

   _____

MORE ABOUT COMMANDS Be an earthquake expert. Write four more commands to say during an earthquake.

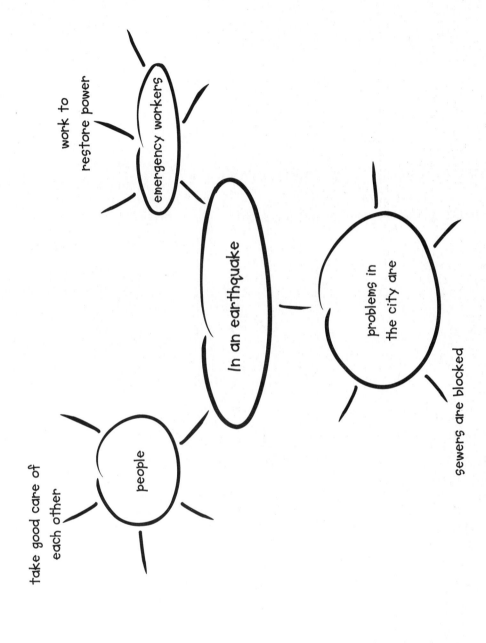

Earthquake Words

Relate Words

DIRECTIONS Work with a group. Sort the new words into the web.

work to
restore power

emergency workers

In an earthquake

problems in
the city are

sewers are blocked

take good care of
each other

people

New Words

epidemic
restore power
rise
ruins
separate
sewer
supplies
take good
care of
tent city
threatened

GRAMMAR: INDEFINITE ADJECTIVES AND ORDINALS

First Things First

DIRECTIONS Study the diagram. Complete the paragraph.
Use order words.

The _____first_____ layer of the Earth is called the *crust*. It is
1.

made of hard rock. The *mantle* is the _____ layer. It is
2.

made up of magma, or melted rock. The *outer core* is actually

deep inside the Earth. This _____ part is
3.

made of liquid metal. At the very center of the Earth

is the _____ layer. The *inner core* is made
4.

of solid metal.

Indefinite Adjectives and Ordinals

Ordinals tell the order of things.
Edith was **first** in line for water.

An adjective can tell how many or how much. Use an **indefinite adjective** when you are not sure of the exact number.
Mr. Somers was buried in **some** beans.

The Earth's Layers

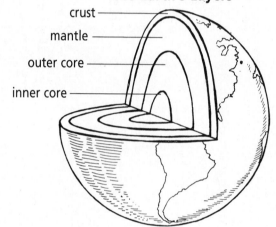

crust —
mantle —
outer core —
inner core —

DIRECTIONS How many beans are circled?
Write the indefinite pronoun.

5.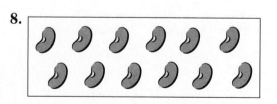

_____

6.

_____

7.

_____

8.

_____

Some Indefinite Adjectives
a few
some
several
many
all

It's a Disaster!

DIRECTIONS Write the contractions. See Handbook page 437 if you need help.

Contractions

A **contraction** is a short way of writing two words. An apostrophe (') shows where letters were left out when the two words were joined.

they are → they're
that is → that's
should not → shouldn't

1. could not   _____couldn't_____

2. do not   _____

3. she would   _____

4. is not   _____

5. did not   _____

6. they are   _____

7. let us   _____

8. I have   _____

9. we will   _____

10. it is   _____

11. they will   _____

12. he is   _____

13. I am   _____

14. you are   _____

DIRECTIONS Write contractions for the words in parentheses.

15. Problems _____don't_____ disappear when an earthquake stops. (**do not**)

16. The 1906 earthquake _____ just one disaster. (**was not**)

17. In San Francisco, the quake _____ do as much damage as the fire. (**did not**)

18. After the quake there _____ enough to eat. (**was not**)

19. People _____ go into their damaged homes. (**could not**)

20. When people hear of disaster, _____ eager to help. (**they are**)

21. _____ why people sent food from all over the country. (**that is**)

22. _____ our responsibility to help others in need. (**it is**)

San Francisco, California. April 18, 1906

See, Hear, and Read All About It!

DIRECTIONS Study each report about the 1906 San Francisco earthquake. Write what you learned from each kind of media. Then answer the questions.

Using Different Media

Writers and reporters use different **media** to describe events. Some examples of media are: photographs, newspaper reports, television news, personal accounts, and Internet postings.

Newspaper

EXTRA THE DAILY NEWS EXTRA

HUNDREDS DEAD!

Fire Follows Earthquake, Laying Downtown Section in Ruins--City Seems Doomed For Lack of Water

KNOWN DEAD AT MECHANICS' PAVILION

Max Fenner, policeman, killed in collapse Essex Hotel.
Niece of Detective Dillon, killed in collapse, 6th and Shipley.
Unidentified woman, killed at 18 7th st.
Two unknown men, brought in autos.

OTHER DEAD

Five killed, 2 injured, in col-

Photograph and Caption

City Hall was destroyed by the earthquake.

Eyewitness Account

"I wake up about 5 o'clock, feeling my bed rocking as though I am in a ship on the ocean...I get up and go to the window, raise the shade and look out. And what I see makes me tremble with fear. I see the buildings toppling over, big pieces of masonry falling, and from the street below I hear the cries and screams of men and women and children."

– Enrico Caruso

1. From this part of a newspaper report, I learned

_____

_____

_____.

2. From this photograph and caption, I learned

_____

_____

_____

_____.

3. From this eyewitness account, I learned

_____

_____

_____

_____.

4. Which medium did you like best? Why?

_____

_____

_____

Rewrite a Play

DIRECTIONS Work with a partner. Follow the steps
to rewrite a scene from "Earthquake at Dawn."

1 **Review the Play** Where and when does the play take place?
Write details about the setting in the chart.

Details	1906	20 _ _
How people dress	women wear petticoats	
How people talk		
How the city looks		
Where it takes place		
Commands people give		
How people help others		

2 **Change the Setting** How would the story be different if the earthquake happened
today? Add new details to the chart.

3 **Choose a Scene** Think about the characters and action in each scene of the play.
Choose one to rewrite.

☐ Scene 1, pages 229–231   ☐ Scene 2, page 232   ☐ Scene 3, pages 234–236

4 **Rewrite the Scene** Use ideas from your chart. Include all the parts of a play. See
the Reading Strategy on page 226 of your book for help.

Volcanoes Can Erupt

DIRECTIONS Read each sentence. Write the helping verb and the main verb.

Some Helping Verbs			
can	could	would	should
may	might	must	will

Helping Verbs

Some verbs are made up of more than one word. A **helping verb** comes before the **main verb.** The main verb shows the action.

An earthquake **can cause** great damage.

In a negative sentence, the word **not** comes between the helping verb and the main verb.

People should **not** run outside.

	Helping Verbs	Main Verbs
1. Inside the earth, rocks can get hot enough to melt.	can	get
2. Melted rock might push through the earth's crust.	_____	_____
3. Ash could shoot miles into the atmosphere.	_____	_____
4. People nearby would not survive the blast.	_____	_____
5. There may be thousands of years between eruptions.	_____	_____
6. We must study volcanoes to keep people safe.	_____	_____

DIRECTIONS Add a helping verb to complete each sentence.

7. A volcano _____may_____ erupt at any time.

8. During an eruption, the top of a mountain _____ collapse.

9. Ash from a volcano _____ cover whole forests.

10. One day, a volcano in the United States _____ erupt again.

11. People _____ be prepared.

12. Good preparation _____ save lives!

In 1980, Mount St. Helens blew its top! This is a photograph of the eruption.

RESEARCH SKILLS

Use Parts of a Book

Table of Contents

DIRECTIONS Study the table of contents from <u>California Quakes!</u>
by Dr. John Jackson. Answer the questions.

The table of contents is in the beginning of the book. It shows the book's general topics. It tells the page numbers for each chapter or section of the book.

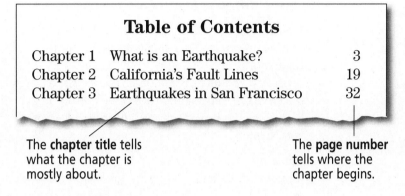

Table of Contents

The **chapter title** tells what the chapter is mostly about.

The **page number** tells where the chapter begins.

1. Which chapter has information about San Francisco earthquakes? _____

2. On what page does Chapter 2 begin? _____

3. Would you use this book to find out about earthquakes in Mexico?

   Why or why not? _____

Index

DIRECTIONS Study the index. Answer the questions.

The index is in the back of the book. It lists specific topics in the book and where you can find information about them.

Topics are listed in alphabetical order.

Sometimes **italics** show there is an illustration on the page.

Related details are often listed for a topic.

Page numbers show you where to find the information.

4. On which pages can you find information about the San Francisco earthquake in 1989? _____

_____

5. Would the entry *Richter Scale* come before or after *San Andreas Fault System*? _____

Article

DIRECTIONS Skim the article from a book. Look quickly at the title, headings, beginning sentences, and picture. Then answer the questions.

32

The 1906 San Francisco Earthquake

Terror Strikes the City

The San Francisco earthquake struck in the early morning on April 18, 1906. More than 700 people were killed. Buildings collapsed across the city. The earthquake registered 7.8 on the Richter scale. It was felt in California, Oregon, and Nevada.

The earthquake destroyed the Hibernia Bank Building.

Aftershocks and Fires

A major aftershock struck the city at 8:14 a.m. Soon afterward, fire broke out all over the city. All morning and early afternoon, fires spread from building to building. The Winchester Hotel caught fire at 11:00 a.m., and collapsed. At noon, the Hearst Building caught fire. The Hibernia Bank Building was also destroyed. Then at 1:00 p.m., St. Mary's Hospital burned to the ground. It was clear that the damage did not end when the shaking stopped.

6. What can you learn from the title and headings? _____

_____

7. What do the picture and caption tell you about the earthquake? _____

_____

8. What happened at 8:14 a.m. on April 18, 1906? _____

_____

9. You want to know what damage the 1906 earthquake did in Oregon. Would you use this article

for your research? Tell why or why not. _____

_____

10. Will the article help you add facts to a time line about the 1906 earthquake? Explain.

_____

_____

Create an Earthquake Data Chart

DIRECTIONS Work with a partner. Research three recent earthquakes.
Follow the steps.

1 **Find Sources** Look up the topic "earthquakes" in newspapers or on the
Internet. Ask your teacher or librarian for help.

2 **Read and Take Notes** Read each article. Look for the main facts about
each earthquake. Take notes in the data chart. Be sure to write the sources
for your information.

Earthquake Data Chart

Earthquake	Location	Date	Size	Damage
Earthquake 1				
Earthquake 2				
Earthquake 3				

3 **Compare Earthquakes** Show your chart to the class. Tell how the
earthquakes are the same. Tell how they are different.

BUILD LANGUAGE AND VOCABULARY

Tell More About It

DIRECTIONS Complete the sentences. Choose adjectives, adverbs, and prepositional phrases to tell more about the picture.

Adjectives	Adverbs	Prepositional Phrases
tall	carefully	up the sides
hard	soon	to the top
heavy	slowly	before dark
brave	calmly	near the top
large	completely	under the pile
empty	safely	down the sides
destructive	now	in the daytime
broken	wearily	for protection
tired	later	on their heads

Adjectives, Adverbs, Prepositions

An **adjective** describes a person, place, or thing.
   Helpful people lift **heavy** sandbags.

An **adverb** tells how, where, or when.
   Nearby, a wall of sandbags **slowly** forms.

A **preposition** can help to show location, direction, time, and other details. A **prepositional phrase** starts with a preposition. It ends with a noun or pronoun.
   Tired workers lean **against the wall**.

Workers clean up after a strong earthquake.

1. People clean up _____in the daytime_____ after a

   _____destructive_____ earthquake.

2. They wear _____ hats

   _____ .

3. Some _____ people search

   _____ .

4. They work _____ and

   _____ .

5. They fill _____ buckets with

   _____ concrete.

6. Others carry _____ buckets _____ .

7. The _____ crane lifts _____
   pieces of concrete.

8. The _____ workers want to finish the

   job _____ .

After the Disaster

New Words

aid
damage
evacuee
recovery
relief worker
rescue worker
shelter
struggle
survivor
wreckage

Use New Words in Context

DIRECTIONS Study the diagram. Use the new words to write a paragraph about disasters.

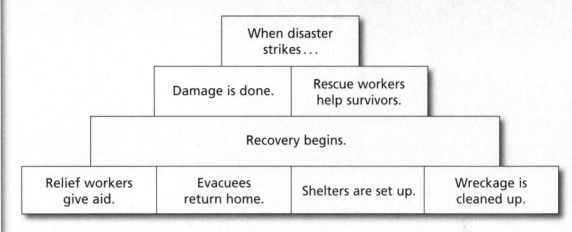

When Disaster Strikes

Tell the main idea in your **topic sentence**.	_____ _____ _____
Give **details**. Tell what happens when disaster strikes.	_____ _____ _____
Give **details**. Tell what happens when recovery begins.	_____ _____ _____
Sum up your paragraph. Write a **concluding sentence**.	_____ _____

City Shakes Violently!

DIRECTIONS Write the correct form of the adverb to complete the sentence. See Handbook page 428 for help.

1. The earthquake struck **hard**.

   The earthquake struck _____ harder _____ than any other.

2. The ground shook **violently** at first.

   The ground shook _____

   after the first few seconds.

3. The death toll was **high**.

   The death toll went _____ each day.

4. Buildings fell **easily**.

   Tall buildings fell _____ than small buildings.

5. After the quake, rescuers worked **fast**.

   Some rescuers worked _____ than others.

6. People dug **urgently** in the rubble.

   People dug the _____ for loved ones.

7. Medical teams arrived **soon**. Some doctors arrived

   _____ than others.

8. Aid came **quickly** from around the world.

   Aid came _____

   than for other quakes.

> ### Adverbs That Compare
>
> Some adverbs compare two or more actions.
>
> Add **–er** to compare two actions.
>   Sara dug **faster** than Ryan.
>
> Add **–est** to compare three or more actions.
>   Francisco dug the **fastest** of all.
>
> If the adverb ends in **–ly**, use **more**, **most**, **less**, or **least**.
>   Ryan dug **more carefully** than the others.

The earth shook violently in San Francisco, California, in 1989. Many buildings, like this one, were destroyed.

You Can't Count the Damage

DIRECTIONS Work with a partner. Look for plural nouns in the news article on pages 246 and 247 of your book. Write each noun in the correct column in the chart.

> ## Count and Noncount Nouns
>
> A **count noun** names something you can count. It has a singular and a plural form:
>
> 1 jug → 2 **jugs**
> 1 person → 2 **people**
> 1 city → 2 **cities**
>
> A **noncount noun** names something you cannot count. It does not have a plural form.
>
> **Aid** came in from all over.
> Planes brought in **water**.

Count Nouns	Noncount Nouns
miles	air

MORE ABOUT NOUNS Look at your list of noncount nouns in the chart. Do they tell about weather, materials, or food? Make another chart. Write the noncount nouns where they belong. Add other noncount nouns in each category.

Example:

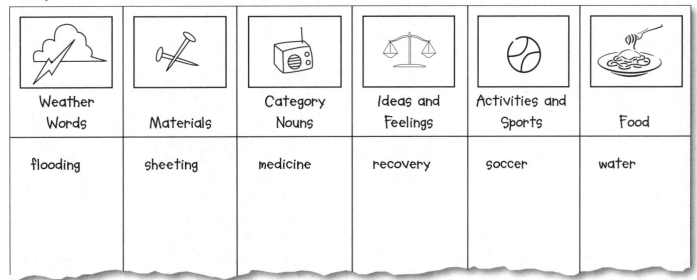

Weather Words	Materials	Category Nouns	Ideas and Feelings	Activities and Sports	Food
flooding	sheeting	medicine	recovery	soccer	water

River Rises Rapidly

DIRECTIONS Read the article. Underline the adverbs that tell *how*.

Residents Flee as River Rises

The Red River continued to rise <u>swiftly</u> today. Volunteers worked urgently to fill and pile sandbags. In spite of their efforts, the river rapidly washed away the wall. Eventually, federal aid will help people.

Residents hit by floods last week have already started to clean up.

One victim spoke honestly about his loss. "We tried earnestly to save our things. In the end, we had to run quickly to save our lives." He hugged his son warmly. "Our family is staying at a shelter. We're all safe. That's what counts," he said, sincerely.

DIRECTIONS Use an adverb to complete each sentence. Add *–ly* to the word in parentheses.

1. It rained _____constantly_____ all week. (**constant**)

2. The river rose _____ . (**swift**)

3. Residents _____ packed valuables and family portraits. (**quick**)

4. People drove _____ away from their homes. (**careful**)

5. Volunteers worked _____ . (**urgent**)

6. The river _____ washed away the wall of sandbags. (**rapid**)

7. Many families stayed _____ with friends or relatives. (**brief**)

8. At least they could sleep _____ indoors. (**safe**)

9. People spoke _____ about their losses. (**honest**)

10. Federal aid will arrive _____ . (**eventual**)

Make Comparisons

DIRECTIONS Compare an earthquake and a flood.
Use the Venn diagram.

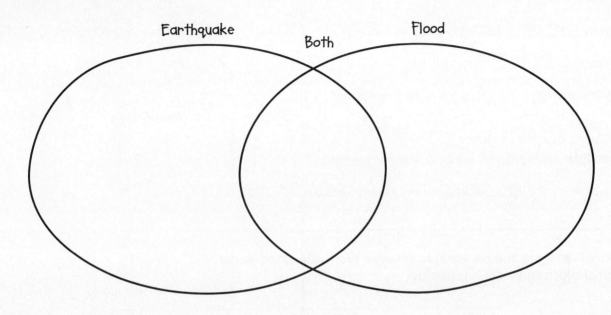

Earthquake   Both   Flood

DIRECTIONS Write a paragraph to compare an earthquake
and a flood. Use the details from your Venn diagram.

Write a **topic sentence**.
Tell what two disasters
you will compare.

_____

_____

_____

Write **details** to tell
how the disasters are
the same or different.
Use **comparison
words** such as *both*
and *alike*, or *unlike*
and *but.*

_____

_____

_____

_____

_____

_____

_____

Write a **concluding
sentence**. Are the
two disasters more
alike than
different? Explain.

_____

_____

_____

_____

Disaster Watch

DIRECTIONS Read each sentence. Circle the correct helping verb.

1. The rain __(is)/ are__ falling heavily in Oregon.

2. The rivers __is / are__ rising rapidly.

3. Many volunteers __is / are__ stacking sandbags.

4. The community center __is / are__ preparing a shelter.

5. The people __is / are__ buying emergency supplies.

6. The mayor __is / are__ telling people to stay calm.

Helping Verbs

The words **is** and **are** are **helping verbs**. Use them with verbs that end in **–ing** to show that an action is still happening.

Use **is** to tell about one person or thing.

The ground **is** shaking.

Use **are** for more than one person or thing.

The people **are** working together.

DIRECTIONS Rewrite the paragraph. Change the underlined verbs. Show that the action is still happening.

> Mr. Inouye's class studies disasters. The students work in groups. Paola's group goes to the library. Paola reads magazine articles about hurricanes. Noel and Joey learn about earthquakes. They draw a map to show earthquake locations. Rosa searches the Internet. She records information about floods around the world.

Mr. Inouye's class is studying disasters.

_____

_____

_____

_____

_____

_____

_____

LANGUAGE ARTS: PREFIXES AND SUFFIXES

Helpless Against a Flood

Tireless volunteers used small boats to get people to safety.

Prefixes and Suffixes

A **prefix** comes at the beginning of a word. The prefix **re–** means "again."

Ingrid waited for the sun to **reappear**.

A **suffix** comes at the end of a word. The suffix **–less** means "without." The suffix **–ous** means "full of."

People are **homeless**.

The work is **dangerous**.

DIRECTIONS Complete each sentence. Use the meaning to write a new word that has a prefix or a suffix.

1. Residents were _____helpless_____ against the rising water.
   without help

2. The situation seemed _____ .
   without hope

3. Then _____ volunteers came from all over the county.
   without fear

4. No one was _____ .
   without care

5. Still, the situation was too _____ for volunteers.
   full of danger

6. The firefighters were very _____ .
   full of courage

7. They tried to _____ the water away from the houses.
   direct again

8. "I don't want to _____ this experience," said one resident.
   live through again

9. "Many people are _____ ."
   without a home

10. "We will have to _____ our lives."
    build again

© Hampton-Brown

Explore Geography

DIRECTIONS Follow the steps to make a disaster map.

1 **Collect Information** Research earthquakes, hurricanes, and floods around the world. Use an almanac or Web sites. Take notes in a chart like this one.

Disasters

Source	Disaster	Location	Date
www.tropicsweather.com/ andrew.html	Hurricane Andrew	Homestead, Florida	August 24, 1992

2 **Make a Map** Draw or trace a map. Show the countries or continents where the disasters happened.

3 **Mark the Map** Make a symbol for each disaster. Use the symbols to mark the location of each disaster on the map. Write each location and date. Your map might look like this:

4 **Share Your Map** Display your map. Talk to your class about it. Do they see any patterns about where disasters happen?

UNIT 5 MIND MAP

Traditions

DIRECTIONS Use the mind map to write about the tradition of storytelling. Read each selection in the unit. Add to the map ideas you learn about storytelling.

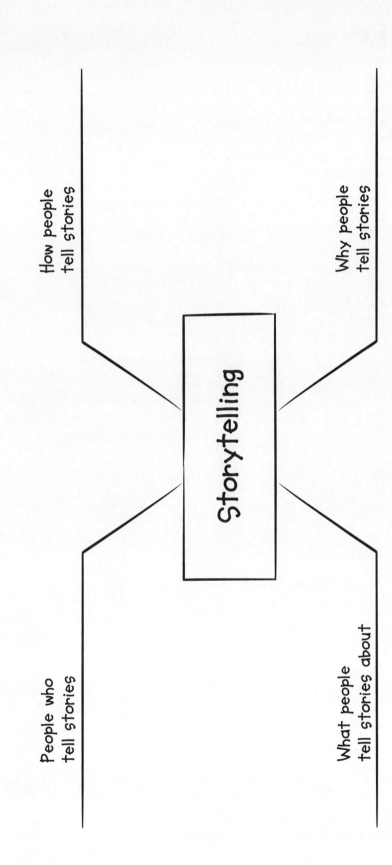

How people
tell stories

Why people
tell stories

Storytelling

People who
tell stories

What people
tell stories about

BUILD LANGUAGE AND VOCABULARY

Describing the Greek Gods

DIRECTIONS Work with a partner. Read "The Mount Olympus Rap" on page 266 of your book. Then read the subjects and predicates below. Draw lines to match the subjects with their predicates.

> **Complete Sentences**
>
> Every **complete sentence** has a subject and a predicate. The **subject** tells whom or what the sentence is about. The **predicate** tells what the subject is, has, or does.
>
> <u>Ancient Greeks</u> <u>told myths about their gods.</u>
>   subject   predicate

Subjects	Predicates
1. The ancient Greeks	was named Zeus.
2. Mount Olympus	had twelve children.
3. Chaos	believed in many gods.
4. Earth Mother Gaia	made the flowers bloom.
5. Old Cronus	created the heavens and the earth.
6. The gods and goddesses	was one of Gaia's children.
7. The powerful king of the gods	was home to the gods.
8. The beautiful Aphrodite	got along sometimes.

DIRECTIONS Add a subject or a predicate to complete each sentence.

9. Zeus and Hera _____ married.

10. _____ had a son named Ares.

11. Ares _____ .

12. _____ protected the Greek cities.

13. The gods and goddesses _____ .

14. The fascinating stories _____ .

MORE ABOUT COMPLETE SENTENCES Write subjects. Have a partner write complete sentences by adding a predicate to each subject.

The Greeks called the Earth Mother "Gaia." She had twelve children called the Titans.

Words That Tell a Story

New Words

adorable

attendant

disrespectful

echo

pine

repeat

took pity

wept

wood nymph

Use New Words in Context

DIRECTIONS Read the myth. Add the new words.

There once was a _____wood nymph_____ who found a baby. She
                              1.

_____ on the lonely child. Her _____ helped
        2.   **3.**

care for the sweet, _____ baby. The baby tried to
                              4.

_____ every word he heard. He liked the _____ .
        5.   **6.**

When the baby grew into a man, the wood nymph said, "You must go to the human

world." He _____ and cried, but was never _____ .
              7.   **8.**

His tears made a stream through the woods. "Don't _____ ," said
                                                            9.

the wood nymph. "You can follow the stream whenever you want to return to me."

Relate Words

DIRECTIONS Work with a partner. Find pairs of new words that go together
in some way. Then complete each sentence.

10. _____Echo_____ and _____repeat_____ go together because

____an echo repeats a sound_____ .

11. _____ and _____ go together because

_____ .

12. _____ and _____ go together because

_____ .

13. _____ and _____ go together because

_____ .

14. _____ and _____ go together because

_____ .

Investigating Characters

DIRECTIONS Read the character traits and motives in the chart. Write which character from "Echo and Narcissus" they tell about.

	Character	Traits	Motives
1.		powerful irritable	wants to teach a lesson wants to be respected
2.		talkative loving	wants to have the last word wants to be noticed
3.		selfish frightened	wants to be alone wants to get away

> ### Character Traits and Motives
>
> A **character trait** tells what the character is like.
>
> > Hera is **powerful** and **strong**.
>
> A **character's motive** tells why the character does something.
>
> > Hera punishes Echo **to show her power**.

DIRECTIONS Use the chart to write sentences about each character's traits and motives.

4. Hera is _powerful_____ .

   She wants _to teach Echo a lesson_____ ,

   so she _punishes Echo for talking_____ .

5. Echo is _____ .

   She wants _____ ,

   so she _____ .

6. Narcissus is _____ .

   He wants _____ ,

   so he _____ .

MORE ABOUT TRAITS AND MOTIVES Work with a partner. Choose a character from a story in this unit. Discuss the character's traits and motives.

Figure Out the Outcome

Goal and Outcome

The **goal** is what a character wants. The **outcome** tells if the goal is reached.

- An **intended outcome** happens when a character reaches the goal.
- An **unintended outcome** is when something happens that the character does not expect.

DIRECTIONS Work with a partner. Read each character's goal. Then tell about the outcomes of the character's action.

Goals and Outcomes

Character's Goal	Intended Outcome	Unintended Outcome
Hera wants to teach Echo a lesson.	Echo can't speak her own words.	Echo falls in love but can't express herself.
Echo wants to talk to Narcissus.		
Narcissus wants to touch the beautiful face in the pool.		
Aphrodite wants to show pity for Narcissus.		

DIRECTIONS Were the characters happy with the outcomes? Write sentences about each character's goals and outcomes.

1. Hera _was unhappy with the outcome. She punished Echo, but later she felt sorry for her_ .

2. Echo _____
   _____ .

3. Narcissus _____
   _____ .

4. Aphrodite _____
   _____ .

GRAMMAR: PHRASES

Snapshots of Ancient Greece

DIRECTIONS Read the caption for each picture.
Underline each prepositional phrase.

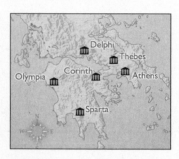

1. Ancient Greece was a
   collection of city-states.
   They were all near the
   Mediterranean Sea.

2. Pericles lived in the 5th
   century, BCE. He talked
   about democracy. He said,
   "Everyone is equal before
   the law."

3. Tourists stand outside
   ancient Greek buildings.
   They take pictures with
   their cameras.

DIRECTIONS Write a caption for each picture. Use complete
sentences. Include prepositional phrases.

Greek Buildings

Athena

4. _____

   _____

   _____

   _____

5. _____

   _____

   _____

   _____

Monitor Your Reading

DIRECTIONS Read the fable. As you read, complete the activities in the chart.

The Raven Bridge

Long ago, there was a beautiful young princess. The princess lived in the sky. She showed great generosity to all the animals. Every day, she gave the hungry black ravens bread from her table.

The princess loved a poor shepherd. The emperor did not want the princess and the shepherd to marry. He sent the princess to one side of a river. Then he banished the shepherd to the other side.

Once a year, the ravens fly into the sky. They build a bridge across the river. Then the princess and the shepherd walk across the bridge. They meet again.

Even now, on the seventh day of the seventh month, the ravens disappear from Vietnam. It is said that the princess and the shepherd are meeting. Their tears of joy bring life to the dry earth.

Visualize:
Describe or draw the pictures the story makes you see in your mind.

Clarify:
Write any unfamiliar words. Ask yourself:
How are the words used in the sentences? What do they mean?

Paraphrase:
Retell the fable in your own words.

GRAMMAR: COMPLETE SENTENCES

The First Democracy

DIRECTIONS Read each sentence. Draw one line under the complete subject. Draw two lines under the complete predicate.

1. Modern democracy began in ancient Greece.

2. It began around 500 BCE.

3. Citizens met to make laws.

4. A council of 500 men held meetings every day.

5. They decided on things to discuss.

6. The Greeks believed in justice.

7. A voting system let people choose leaders.

8. Ten elected generals protected Athens from attack.

9. Athenian citizens voted secretly.

10. The people called their system of government *demokratia*.

Complete Sentences

A **complete sentence** has a subject and a predicate. The subject tells whom or what the sentence is about. The **complete subject** includes all the words in the subject.

Ancient Greek city-states made their own laws.

The predicate tells what the subject is, has, or does. The **complete predicate** includes all the words in the predicate.

The Greeks **believed strongly in personal liberty**.

DIRECTIONS Read "Life in Ancient Greece," on pages 274-275 of your book. Then complete each sentence. Add a subject or a predicate.

11. Delphi, Thebes, and Athens _were all Greek city-states_____ .

12. _____ shared the same language.

13. The city of Athens _____ .

14. The first democracy _____ .

15. People in ancient Greece _____ .

16. _____ controlled people's lives.

MORE ABOUT COMPLETE SENTENCES Write complete sentences about Greece or the Greek gods. Draw one line under the complete subject. Draw two lines under the complete predicate.

© Hampton-Brown

Compare Governments

DIRECTIONS Compare the governments of ancient Greece and the United States. Follow the steps.

1 **Review the Article** Look back at "Life in Ancient Greece." Answer the questions in the chart.

2 **Do Research** Find information about the United States government. Look in encyclopedias, social studies books, or on the Internet. Add notes to the chart.

3 **Discuss Your Findings** Talk with a partner. Explain how the governments are the same and how they are different.

Democracy in Ancient Greece and the United States

Questions	Ancient Greece	United States
When did democracy begin?	Democracy began around 500 BCE.	Democracy began in 1776.
Where do the people live?		
How do they choose leaders?		
How are people punished?		
How can the laws be changed?		
What does the law protect?		

BUILD LANGUAGE AND VOCABULARY

Comparing Reports

DIRECTIONS Read each compound sentence. Underline the two main ideas. Then circle the word that joins the two ideas.

> **Compound Sentences**
>
> A **compound sentence** is made up of two sentences. The two sentences are usually joined by a comma and the word **and**, **but**, or **or**.
>
> Delia studied ancient China.
> Ving studied ancient Greece.
> Delia studied ancient China, **but** Ving studied ancient Greece.

1. Jesús was born in Mexico, (but) he decided to study Greece.

2. Jesús found an ancient map, and Ving found some pictures.

3. Delia and Hee Sun wanted to make a video about China, but they needed to do some research.

4. The girls could use books, or they could search the Internet.

In the 1970s, 6,000 life-sized Terra Cotta Warriors were discovered in China. They had been burried since 206 BCE.

DIRECTIONS Join each pair of sentences to make a compound sentence. Use a comma and the word *and*, *but*, or *or*.

5. The class gave presentations. Delia and Hee Sun went first.

   The class gave presentations, and Delia and Hee Sun went first.
   _____

6. The students could watch from their desks. They could sit on the floor.

   _____
   _____

7. The girls put in their video. The VCR would not work.

   _____
   _____

8. Jesús helped them. Soon the video played perfectly.

   _____
   _____

Workers in the Field

Locate and Use Definitions

New Words

blessing

crop

harvest time

labor

peasant

plow

sundown

sunup

thick

DIRECTIONS Look up the definitions for each new word in the Glossary. Then complete the word web.

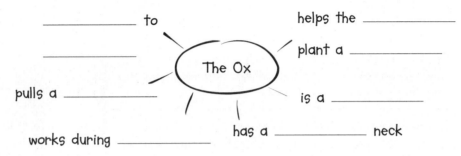

must labor from

_____ to

_____

pulls a _____

works during _____

The Ox

helps the _____

plant a _____

is a _____

has a _____ neck

Use New Words in Context

DIRECTIONS Write a paragraph about the ox. Use the new words.

_____

_____

_____

_____

_____

_____

_____

_____

_____

_____

_____

_____

A Chinese Myth

DIRECTIONS Read the rules for compound sentences. Then use *and*, *but*, or *or* to join the sentence pairs.

Word	Rule	Example
and	Use **and** to join two ideas that are alike.	Lily Toy Hong retold an old Chinese myth in a book, **and** she won an award for it.
but	Use **but** to show how two ideas are different.	The myth began in China, **but** now people all over the world know it.
or	Use **or** to show a choice between two ideas.	You can read the story in a book, **or** you can hear it from a storyteller.

Compound Sentences

A **compound sentence** is made up of two sentences. The two sentences are usually joined by a comma and the word **and**, **but**, or **or**.

The story is old. It is our favorite.
The story is old, **but** it is our favorite.

1. In the beginning, there were no oxen on Earth.
They could be found in the heavens.

   In the beginning, there were no oxen on Earth, but they could be found in the heavens.

   _____

2. The Emperor lived in the Imperial Palace. The oxen lived there, too.

   _____

   _____

3. The oxen wore beautiful silk robes. They reclined all day on soft, fluffy clouds.

   _____

   _____

4. The oxen had easy lives. The peasants on Earth did not.

   _____

   _____

5. Everyone had to honor the Emperor. They would be punished.

   _____

   _____

What Is It Like?

DIRECTIONS Read the description. Then complete the word web. Add words that tell how things look, sound, feel, smell, or taste.

Description

A **description** tells what a person, place, or thing is like. Many descriptions use **sensory words** to tell how things look, sound, feel, smell, and taste.

A Village Celebration

The Chinese peasants celebrate the harvest. They decorate the village with red and green cloth. They prepare ten tables piled high with food and fragrant flowers. The fried rice is colorful and the vegetables are steaming hot. For dessert, each person has a sticky, sweet cake. People can smell the delicious food for miles around.

After dinner, a bright red dragon dances. The dragon has shining gold ribbons. Musicians beat huge drums. They play a loud, low rhythm. The people cheer and clap. They set off noisy firecrackers. The air is filled with smoke. They celebrate the end of the long, hard harvest.

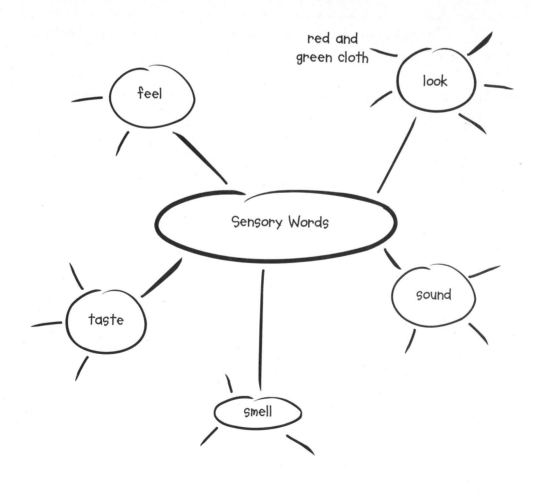

red and green cloth

look

feel

Sensory Words

taste

smell

sound

LITERARY ANALYSIS: FANTASY AND REALITY

Is It Real or Not?

The Ox Star lived in the heavens.

Oxen live on the Earth.

Fantasy and Reality

Fantasy tells about things that cannot happen in real life.
  The ox wears silk robes.

Reality tells about people, places, things, and events that are real.
  Chen steers the oxen.

DIRECTIONS Think about the details in "How the Ox Star Fell from Heaven" and "A Peasant's Life in Ancient China." Write the elements of fantasy and reality in each selection.

Characters or Events	Fantasy Elements	Reality Elements
Ox Star	Oxen lived in the Imperial Palace of the heavens.	Oxen lived on Earth in ancient China.
Emperor of All the Heavens		
Peasant farmers worked hard.		
Oxen live on Earth.		
The lives of peasant farmers got better.		

MORE ABOUT FANTASY AND REALITY Work with a partner. Choose a fact from the article about ancient China on pages 286–287 of your book. Write a fantasy story based on the fact.

© Hampton-Brown

Identify Sequence of Events

DIRECTIONS Complete the sequence chart for "How the Ox Star Fell from Heaven."

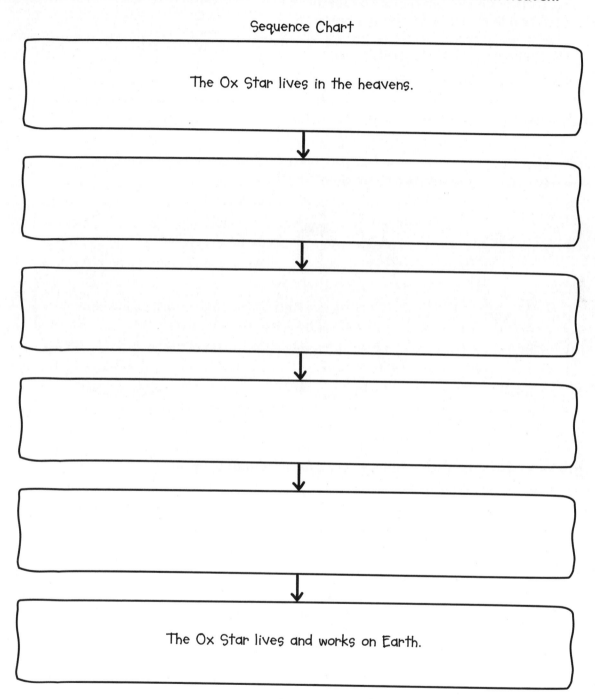

Sequence Chart

The Ox Star lives in the heavens.

The Ox Star lives and works on Earth.

DIRECTIONS Talk about your chart with a partner. Which parts of the myth are based on facts? Make a list of the events that agree with facts from "A Peasant's Life in Ancient China."

They Worked Together

Complete Sentences

A **complete sentence** has a subject and a predicate. The **simple subject** is the most important word in the **complete subject**.

My friend **May** was born in China.

The **simple predicate** is the verb in the **complete predicate**.

May **lived** in China for 12 years.

DIRECTIONS Read each sentence. Draw one line under the simple subject. Draw two lines under the simple predicate.

1. My ancestors in China were hard-working peasants.

2. They worked day and night in the fields.

3. The strong men used oxen to prepare the fields.

4. Then the women in the family planted the seeds.

5. The whole family gathered the rice at harvest time.

DIRECTIONS Add a simple subject or a simple predicate to complete each sentence. Tell which part of the sentence you added.

6. Strong _____oxen_____ are helpful in planting and harvesting crops.   ___subject___

7. Their strong shoulders _____ plows for farmers.   _____

8. The sharp _____ cut through the hard earth.   _____

9. The farmers carefully _____ seeds into the rows.   _____

10. The plants _____ steadily throughout the season.   _____

11. Later, the _____ harvest the ripe plants.   _____

12. The helpful _____ pull wagons filled with crops.   _____

MORE ABOUT COMPLETE SENTENCES Write complete sentences about your ancestors or your family. Draw one line under the simple subject. Draw two lines under the simple predicate.

GRAMMAR: COMPOUND SENTENCES

Farming in China

DIRECTIONS Write compound sentences. Combine the independent clauses with a comma and the word *and*, *but*, or *or*.

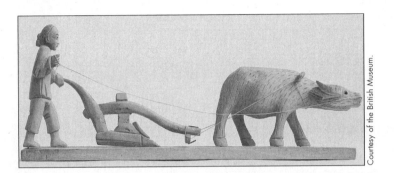

Courtesy of the British Museum.

> ### Compound Sentences
>
> A **clause** is a group of words with a subject and a verb. An **independent clause** can stand alone as a sentence.
>
> > Some farmers use machinery.
> > Some farmers rely on oxen.
>
> When you join two independent clauses, you make a **compound sentence**. The clauses can be joined by a comma and the word **and**, **but**, or **or**.
>
> > Some farmers use machinery, **but** others rely on oxen.

1. China has a lot of land. Not all of it is good for growing crops.

   China has a lot of land, but not all of it is good for growing crops.
   _____

2. Chinese farmers must produce a good harvest. Many people will suffer.

   _____

   _____

3. Oxen help some farmers in their fields. It is still difficult work.

   _____

   _____

4. In southern China, rice is the most important crop. In the north, wheat is more important.

   _____

   _____

5. In central China, farmers can grow rice. They can grow wheat.

   _____

   _____

6. Chinese farmers also grow many other crops. They share their produce with the world.

   _____

   _____

Representing Information

DIRECTIONS Read about graphic organizers on pages 340–347 in the Handbook. Then write what each organizer shows.

Map

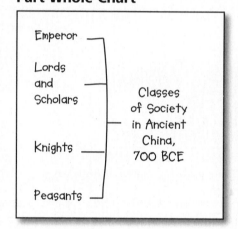

This map shows where

_____ was

located compared to

_____ .

Part-Whole Chart

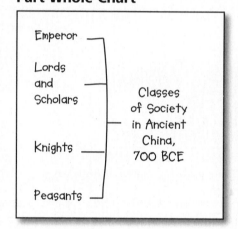

This chart shows that _____

_____

_____ are parts of

_____ .

Word Web

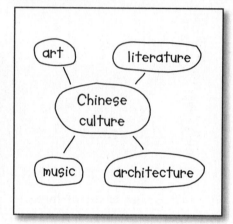

The word web shows how

_____

are related.

Sequence Chart

This sequence chart shows the

time order for _____

_____ .

Venn Diagram

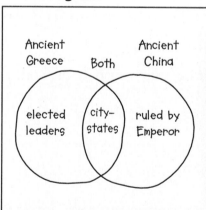

The diagram shows some

between _____

_____ .

Cause-and-Effect Chart

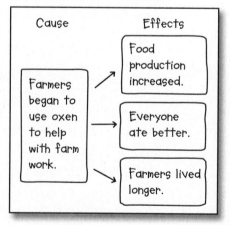

This chart shows how

caused _____

_____ .

© Hampton-Brown

DIRECTIONS Work with a partner. Look through your student book and
other textbooks. Find examples of graphic organizers. Complete the chart.

Graphic Organizers

Location	What the Graphic Organizer Looks Like	Type	What it Shows
High Point, page 286	Modern China	Map	This map shows where modern China is located.

Study Modern China

DIRECTIONS Work with a group. Complete the planner for your research and presentation.

Research Planner

Our Group Topic: _____

My Job:

☐ leader ☐ researcher ☐ artist ☐ other:

☐ note-taker ☐ writer ☐ audio-visual expert _____

Sources of Information:

☐ encyclopedia _____

☐ interview _____

☐ almanac _____

☐ map _____

☐ book _____

☐ Internet _____

Key Words for Searches:

_____ _____ _____

Resources for Presentation:

☐ map ☐ video ☐ chart ☐ audio tape

☐ diagram ☐ poster ☐ photographs ☐ other _____

As the Story Is Told . . .

DIRECTIONS Read about another famous person in the Jewish tradition. Read each sentence and circle the dependent clause. Then write the conjunction.

Storytellers like Sarah Ross retell old stories.

Complex Sentences

A **complex sentence** has an independent clause and a dependent clause. An **independent clause** can stand alone as a sentence. A **dependent clause** cannot. A dependent clause usually begins with a word like **if**, **when**, or **because**.

The girl smiled **as** she told her story.
independent clause/dependent clause

A Few Conjunctions		
after	before	so
when	while	as
because	since	

Conjunction

1. I read of David and Goliath
   (before I heard "King Solomon and the Smell of Bread.") _before_

2. David was a shepherd when he was a young boy. _____

3. He had to protect a flock of sheep
   because lions and bears often killed them. _____

4. David's seven brothers fought in King Saul's army
   while David took care of the sheep. _____

5. Early one morning, David took ten loaves of bread to his brothers
   so they would have something good to eat. _____

6. David noticed something strange after he entered the army's camp. _____

7. A giant named Goliath yelled insults while King Saul's army did nothing. _____

8. David offered to fight Goliath because he was not afraid. _____

9. King Saul was hesitant since David was only a young shepherd. _____

10. David challenged the angry giant as he reached for his slingshot. _____

11. David felt confident when he aimed a rock at Goliath. _____

12. David defeated the giant because he was wise and fearless. _____

Words for a Storyteller

New Words

absolute truth

audience

believable

cause

effect

exaggerated

humor

insist

logic

outlandish

Relate Words

DIRECTIONS Draw a line to match the beginning of each sentence with its ending. Then write the sentences.

Beginning

1. An **exaggerated** event is

2. You **insist** that you are not lying

3. A rainstorm was the **cause** and

4. The **audience** laughed at

5. An **outlandish** tale

Ending

and that it is the **absolute truth**.

the storyteller's **humor**.

funny, but not **believable**.

has its own funny **logic**.

a flood was the **effect**.

6. _____

_____

7. _____

_____

8. _____

_____

9. _____

_____

10. _____

_____

MORE ABOUT NEW WORDS Work with a partner. Call out each new word. Have your partner paraphrase its definition.

GRAMMAR: COMPLEX SENTENCES

If You Use Your Imagination . . .

Complex Sentences

A **complex sentence** has an independent clause and a dependent clause. In some complex sentences, **if** begins the dependent clause and **then** begins the independent clause.

<u>**If** I had a giant peach,</u> <u>**then** I would make 100 pies!</u>
dependent clause   independent clause

DIRECTIONS Finish the dependent clauses to complete each complex sentence.

1. If I could fly, then

   I would fly to the stars _____ .

2. If I discover a gold mine, then _____ .

3. If I could be any animal, then _____ .

4. If I was Pecos Bill, then _____ .

DIRECTIONS Write dependent clauses using *if*. Get your ideas from "Pecos Bill." Then trade papers with a partner. Have your partner complete each independent clause. Draw a picture to illustrate each sentence.

5. If _____

   _____ ,

   then _____

   _____

   _____ .

6. If _____

   _____ ,

   then _____

   _____

   _____ .

LITERARY ANALYSIS: SETTING

When and Where

DIRECTIONS Complete the chart. Tell about the setting for "Pecos Bill."

Section Title	Time	Place
1. The Early Life of Pecos Bill (page 300)	when Pecos Bill was born	New England
2. Pecos Bill Grows Up (page 301)	when Pecos Bill was growing up	
3. Pecos Bill Becomes a Cowboy (page 302)		

DIRECTIONS Use the new setting to make up a new episode for "Pecos Bill." Draw pictures and write captions to show the new events.

New Time: the year 2025

New Place: an unknown planet

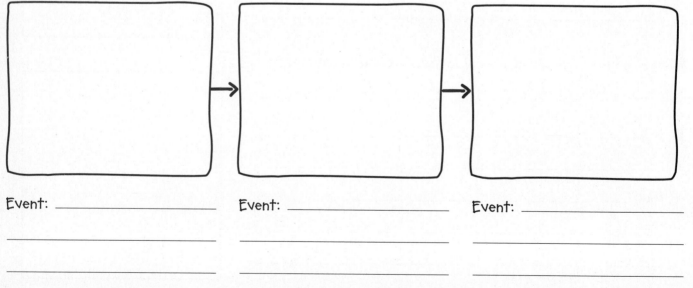

Event: _____   Event: _____   Event: _____

_____   _____   _____

_____   _____   _____

© Hampton-Brown

Use a Time Line to Retell a Tale

DIRECTIONS Follow the steps to retell "Pecos Bill."

1 Complete the time line. Show the events in "Pecos Bill."

First, Bill was born in New England.

Then, his family moved to the Pecos River.

2 Use the time line to help you retell "Pecos Bill" to a partner and to your family. Ask questions to find out what your listeners thought about the tall tale.

- Which part of the tall tale did you like best? Why?
- Which part of the tall tale did you like least? Why?
- Which part of the tall tale was the funniest?
- What would you change in the tall tale?

3 Write sentences to synthesize your listeners' thoughts.

1. My partner thought _____

_____

_____

2. My family thought _____

_____

_____

GRAMMAR: COMPLEX SENTENCES

I Know Because
I Was There!

DIRECTIONS Work with a partner. Add a dependent clause to finish each complex sentence. Begin with a conjunction from the box. Look for ideas on pages 300–302 of your book.

> ### Complex Sentences
> A **complex sentence** has an independent and a dependent clause. An **independent clause** can stand alone as a sentence. A **dependent clause** is not a sentence.
>
> <u>Tall tales are funny</u> <u>because they exaggerate.</u>
>   independent clause   dependent clause
>
> A dependent clause usually begins with a **conjunction** like **if**, **when**, or **because**.
>
> Mr. Larkin tells tall tales **since** people like them.

A Few Conjunctions		
after	before	until
as	since	when
because	so	while

1. Pecos Bill was born _while his Ma was taming a tornado_____.

2. The family moved to Texas _____.

3. The family settled in Texas _____.

4. Bill got lost _____.

DIRECTIONS Work with a partner. Add an independent clause to finish each complex sentence. Circle the conjunction.

5. _Coyotes raised Bill_____

   (since) he was separated from his parents.

6. _____

   because they were beekeepers.

7. _____

   _____

   so they could round up cows.

8. _____

   _____

   after they saw Bill and Joe herding cows.

Using an Atlas

DIRECTIONS Study the index and the map. Then follow the steps to learn about using an atlas.

Atlas

An **atlas** is a book of maps. It has an **index** to help you find maps of continents, countries, and cities.

This shows you where to find a place on the map.

This tells you the page number for the map in the atlas.

Index

Name	Map Reference	Page
Amarillo, Tx., U.S.	A3	256
Amili, China	C8	140
Arlington, Tx., U.S.	C5	256
Arteaga, Mex.	H8	90

The names of places are in alphabetical order.

Use the map reference code to find a place. Find the letter on the side. Look for the number on the bottom. Now find the section where the lettered and numbered spaces meet. Look for the name of the place.

Map

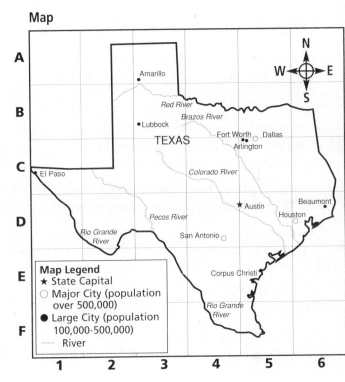

1. **Use the Index** Look in the index to find cities in Texas. Answer the questions.

   • Which page has a map that shows Arlington, Texas? _____

   • Where is Amarillo, Texas located on the map? _____

2. **Locate Cities on the Map** Find Amarillo and Arlington. Circle them.

3. **Find More Information** Look at the legend to see what the symbols on the map mean. Answer the questions.

   • What is the capital city of Texas? _____

   • Write the name of a major city. _____

   • Write the names of the five large rivers you can see on this map. _____

_____

Explore Geography

DIRECTIONS Follow the steps to study the geography of tall tales.

1 List the events in "Pecos Bill."

- Page 300: _____

  _____

- Page 301: _____

  _____

- Page 302: _____

  _____

2 Find the location of each event on the map on the next page, page 161. Write the location and tell what happened there.

3 Study another tall tale. Choose a character. Use encyclopedias, books, or the Internet to learn about the character. Complete the chart.

Character	Location	Events
☐ John Henry		
☐ Annie Oakley		
☐ Paul Bunyan		
☐ Mike Fink		
☐ Other: _____		

4 Write the location of the tall tale on the map. Write the name of the character. Tell about an event from the tale.

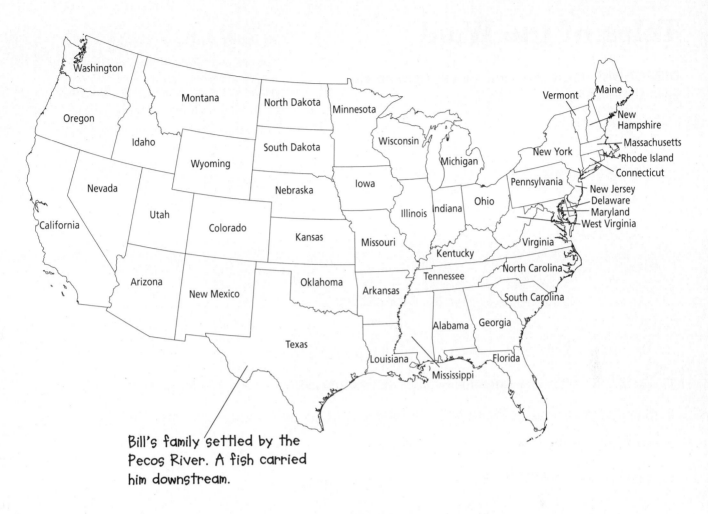

Bill's family settled by the
Pecos River. A fish carried
him downstream.

5 Work with a partner. Brainstorm a new tall tale. Tell the location
and events in the story.

_____

_____

_____

_____

_____

_____

_____

_____

6 Mark the location on the map. Share your tall tale with another pair of students.

BUILD LANGUAGE AND VOCABULARY

Tales of the Wind

DIRECTIONS Circle the correct word to complete each sentence.

> ### Present Perfect Tense
> The **present perfect tense** uses **has** or **have** with an action verb. It can tell about an action that began in the past and may still be going on.
> > The wind **has blown** for days.
>
> It can also tell about an action that began in the past, but you are not sure of the exact time.
> > The trees **have lost** their leaves.
>
> Use **has** for one person, place, or thing.
> Use **have** for more than one.

1. My father _____(has)/ have_____ been a storyteller for many years.

2. He _____**has / have**_____ written many of his stories himself.

3. Some of his stories _____**has / have**_____ come from around the world.

4. My father _____**has / have**_____ told some folk tales many times.

5. Many people _____**has / have**_____ come to hear his stories.

6. Some of his stories _____**has / have**_____ become famous.

DIRECTIONS Write *has* or *have* to complete each sentence.

7. Many cultures _____have_____ enjoyed stories about the wind.

8. People make up stories because no one _____ seen the wind.

9. However, we _____ all felt the wind.

10. In some places, people _____ thrown out oatmeal or flour to feed the hungry wind.

11. In other places, the wind blows because it _____ lost its home.

12. Some people _____ given the wind a name.

13. My father _____ always called the wind "Kookie" in his stories.

14. I _____ always loved my father's stories.

The Storyteller's Craft

New Words

expression

familiar

full attention

gesture

inventiveness

present

respond

talent

Relate Words

DIRECTIONS Use the new words to complete the chart.

show

- a _____ talent _____ for telling stories well.

- _____ because they think up new ways to tell stories.

use

- _____ when they move their bodies.

- their _____ to show feelings.

Talented storytellers

tell

- _____ stories or stories that people already know.

- stories about the past or the _____ .

ask

- audiences to listen and watch with their _____ .

- people to _____ to questions.

Use New Words in Context

DIRECTIONS Write a paragraph about storytellers. Use the chart for ideas.

Storytellers have a talent for telling stories well. _____

_____

_____

_____

_____

_____

_____

_____

GRAMMAR: COMPLEX SENTENCES

Cric? Crac!

DIRECTIONS Read each sentence. Underline the independent clause. Circle the dependent clause.

1. <u>Storyteller Edwidge Danticat has told stories</u> (since she was a little girl.)

2. She lived in Haiti until she was twelve years old.

3. Because her parents moved to New York, she lived with her aunt.

4. After she turned twelve, she joined her parents in Brooklyn.

5. She did not speak much because she was shy.

6. Ms. Danticat's family and her Creole friends supported her when she felt shy and scared.

7. Since she loved Haiti, she wrote about Haitian people and places.

8. Edwidge Danticat named one of her books *Krik? Krak!* because she wanted to honor Haiti's storytelling tradition.

> **Complex Sentences**
>
> A **complex sentence** has an independent clause and a dependent clause. An **independent clause** is a complete sentence. A **dependent clause** is not a sentence.
>
> <u>I will tell a story</u> if you will listen.
> independent clause/dependent clause

Edwidge Danticat is a Haitian American writer. She has written books and short stories about her homeland of Haiti.

DIRECTIONS Complete each complex sentence. Add an independent or dependent clause. Look for ideas on pages 310–311 of "Unwinding the Magic Thread."

9. When the moon is full, _families gather to hear stories_____.

10. _____ if she has a story to share.

11. _____ if the people do not say "Crac!"

12. If the audience wants to listen, _____ .

13. _____ , the audience chooses the storyteller.

14. _____ , the audience gives its full attention.

15. _____ , the audience starts to sing, too.

16. _____ because the storyteller might add something new.

GRAMMAR: PRESENT PERFECT TENSE

A Visit to Haiti

DIRECTIONS Circle the correct word to complete each sentence.

1. Marie-Claire's family _____(has)/ have_____ visited Haiti twice.

2. Her grandparents _____has / have_____ lived there for years.

3. Marie-Claire _____has / have_____ visited the Iron Market in Port au Prince.

4. The city of Port au Prince_____has / have_____ changed over the years.

5. Many people _____has / have_____ moved to the city.

6. The streets _____has / have_____ gotten more crowded.

7. Marie-Claire _____has / have_____ always loved the busy streets.

8. Her grandparents _____has / have_____ been wonderful tour guides!

DIRECTIONS Circle the correct word to complete each sentence. Then underline the past participles.

9. Bernard's class _____(has)/ have_____ studied Haiti.

10. They _____has / have_____ made reports about the country.

11. Jean _____has / have_____ lived in the capital city of Port-au-Prince.

12. He _____has / have_____ taught the class some words in Creole.

13. The students _____has / have_____ grown to love the language.

14. Bernard _____has / have_____ drawn a large map of the Caribbean.

15. Some students _____has / have_____ written letters to Haitian pen pals.

For many years, Haitian artists have sold crafts in Haiti's Iron Market.

Vendors sell many kinds of fruits and vegetables.

Dancing and Clapping

DIRECTIONS Complete each sentence. Use the past progressive form of the verb in parentheses.

> ### Past Progressive
> The **past progressive** form of a verb tells about an action that was happening over a period of time in the past. It uses the helping verb **was** or **were** and an **action verb**. The action verb ends in **–ing**.
> The musicians **were playing**.
> Rooster **was dancing**.

1. Turtle _____ was worrying _____ about the school dance. (**worry**)

2. He _____ very awkward. (**feel**)

3. All his classmates _____ if he would go. (**ask**)

4. Finally, it was Friday night, and music _____ from the hall. (**come**)

5. All his friends _____ . (**dance**)

6. The older folks _____ for them. (**clap**)

7. Turtle _____ outside, afraid to go in. (**wait**)

8. Suddenly, Salamandra _____ beside him. (**stand**)

9. She _____ him to dance! (**ask**)

10. His friends _____ him into the dance hall. (**pull**)

11. His heart _____ . (**pound**)

12. The next thing he knew, he _____ around the floor. (**glide**)

13. His friends _____ for him. (**cheer**)

14. He _____ along with everyone else. (**smile**)

15. Everyone _____ a great time! (**have**)

GRAMMAR: HELPING VERBS

What Does a Storyteller Do?

DIRECTIONS Read the sentences. Draw one line under the helping verbs. Draw two lines under the main verbs.

Helping Verbs

Do and **does** are forms of the helping verb **do**. Use **do** with *I, you, we, they,* and plural nouns.
> **Do** you **like** folk tales?
> I **do like** folk tales.

Use **does** with *he, she, it,* and singular nouns.
> **Does** the story **make** you laugh?
> No, but it **does make** Miguel laugh.

1. <u>Do</u> you <u>like</u> old stories?
   I <u>do</u> <u>like</u> old stories.

2. Do you prefer true stories or fiction?
   Well, a good novel does grab my interest.

3. Does your family tell stories at dinner time?
   No, we do not tell stories at dinner time.

4. Does a funny story make you laugh out loud?
   No, but funny stories do bring a smile to my face.

DIRECTIONS Write a complete sentence to answer each question. Use the helping verb *do* or *does* in each sentence.

5. Does Diane Wolkstein tell folk tales?

   Diane Wolkstein does tell folk tales.
   _____

6. Do some of her folk tales come from Haiti?

   _____

7. Does the story of Owl include songs and dances?

   _____

8. Do you sing along with the songs in "Owl"?

   _____

9. Does "Owl" have a happy ending?

   _____

10. Do you like Diane Wolkstein's stories?

   _____

SUM IT UP

Generate Ideas: New Actions and Outcomes

DIRECTIONS Work with a partner. Choose a character from "Owl." Review your Goal and Outcome charts. In the top row of the map, show what happened in the story. In the bottom row, show what the character should have done to meet the goal. Use words and pictures.

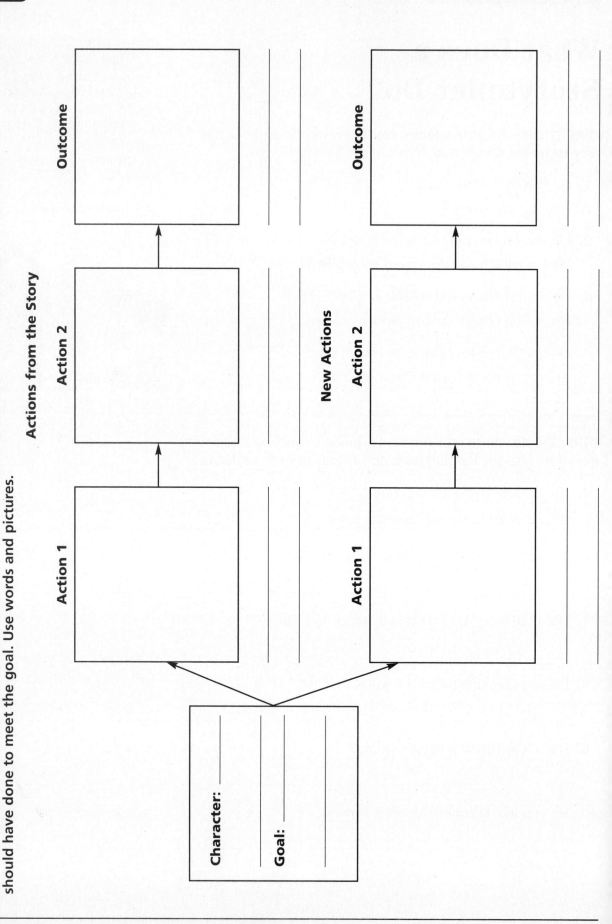

Actions from the Story

| Action 1 | Action 2 | Outcome |

Character: _____

Goal: _____

New Actions

| Action 1 | Action 2 | Outcome |

GRAMMAR: PRESENT PERFECT TENSE

They Have Told Stories

DIRECTIONS Write *has* or *have* to complete each sentence. Draw a line under the past participle.

1. Diane Wolkstein ___has___ told many fascinating tales.

2. People around the world _____ heard them.

3. Some of her stories _____ come from Europe, Israel, and Haiti.

4. Many adults and children _____ enjoyed her work.

5. Ms. Wolkstein _____ written many books.

6. The story of Owl _____ appeared in *The Magic Orange Tree*.

7. Two musicians _____ put "Owl" to music.

8. Ms. Wolkstein _____ encouraged many storytellers.

> **Present Perfect Tense**
>
> The **present perfect tense** can tell about an action that began in the past and may still be going on. It uses the helping verb **has** or **have** and the **past participle** of the main verb.
>
> Ms. Wolkstein **has chosen** a story. She **has memorized** it.

DIRECTIONS Read the article. Circle the verbs in the present perfect tense. Remember to look for actions that may still be going on.

Storyteller Delights Listeners

Winona Tallchief returned to our fair city last week. Once again, she delighted audiences with stories from her Native American heritage. "I have honored my ancestors in my stories," she said to her listeners. "My ancestors have given me a very rich culture. I have been thankful for it all my life."

Ms. Tallchief thrilled her fans as she has thrilled them many times before. Ben White Feather accompanied her tales on flute and drums as he has done in the past.

I spoke with Tallchief after the show. "The stories of my people have inspired me," she said. "I hope to pass on my heritage to others."

Winona Tallchief delighted her audience last Friday with traditional and original stories.

Make a Travel Guide

DIRECTIONS Follow the steps to make a travel guide.

1 Study the page from a travel guide. Then answer the questions.

The **title** tells the name of the country and gets your attention.

This paragraph tells why you should visit the country.

This box shows quick facts about the country.

Haiti: Land of Adventure

Haiti offers exciting adventures to the brave traveler. From exploring beaches and mountains to visiting local markets, you will find that Haiti is a unique destination in the Caribbean.

The **map** shows the location of the country.

Dominican Republic

HAITI

Facts and Figures

Official name: Republic of Haiti
Capital city: Port-au-Prince
Languages: French, Haitian Créole
Currency: Gourde
Population: 7,200,000

Food
The food in Haiti is a blend of West African, French, and Spanish traditions. A typical meal might consist of cod, pork, goat meat, fried plantains, rice, and beans.

Places to See and Things to Do
Haiti offers exciting places to see and things to do. In the capital, Port-au-Prince, you can visit many art galleries. Haitians are famous for their artwork. If you are interested in history, visit The Citadelle LaFerriére, a fortress built in the 1800s.

The **headings** show where you can find specific information about the country.

Climate
Haiti has a tropical climate. The average daytime temperature ranges from 76 to 82 degrees Fahrenheit. It is cooler at night. The rainy season lasts from May to July and then starts again in September through December.

1. What is the title of this article? _____

2. What are the headings in the article? _____

   _____

3. What is the capital of Haiti? _____

4. What does the map tell about Haiti? _____

   _____

5. What colorful words make you want to visit Haiti? _____

   _____

2 **Choose a country for your travel guide.**

I will make a travel guide for _____ .

3 **Find information about the country. Look for facts in an atlas, almanac, encyclopedia, Web site, CD-ROM, or magazine. Take notes.**

Country: _____

Subjects	Notes
location	
climate	
foods	
places to see	
things to do	
special events	

4 **Create your travel guide. Use the travel guide about Haiti as a model. Remember to include:**

☐ a title that catches people's interest   ☐ quick facts about the country

☐ headings that show where to find information   ☐ a map of the country

☐ words that encourage people to visit the country   ☐ photos

5 **Display your travel guide with your classmates' guides. Which places do you want to visit?**

Many Meanings

Use Definitions

DIRECTIONS Read the definitions. Tell how the new word in bold is being used. Write *noun* or *verb*.

New Words

dance

salt

skirt

taste

water

wave

1. A **skirt** is a piece of women's clothing that hangs from the waist. _____noun_____

   When you **skirt** something, you go along its edge. _____

2. A **dance** is a party where people move to music. _____

   When you **dance**, you move to a rhythm. _____

3. You **water** plants to help them grow. _____

   Living things need **water**. _____

4. In the ocean, water comes to the shore in a **wave**. _____

   You **wave** when you move your hand back and forth. _____

5. You **taste** something when you put it in your mouth. _____

   A **taste** of something is a small amount of it. _____

6. **Salt** is a natural product that adds flavor to food. _____

   You can **salt** food to add flavor. _____

Use Context Clues to Meaning

DIRECTIONS Read the paragraph. Circle *noun* or *verb* to show which definition is used for the word on the line.

When I sit on the wall that _____skirts_____ the ocean, memories
                           7. noun / verb

_____dance_____ in my mind. I swam in the _____water_____ when I was
8. noun / verb   **9 noun / verb**

young. I moved back and forth with the _____waves_____. My memories
                                      10. noun / verb

are so strong that I can _____taste_____ the _____salt_____ of the sea.
                        11. noun / verb   **12. noun / verb**

Paraphrase a Poem

DIRECTIONS Work with a partner. Read the poem. Tell your partner what you think each line means. Paraphrase each line in the chart.

> ### The Storyteller
> The storyteller sews a quilt made of scraps and dreams.
> Her voice blooms with a tall yellow flower of joy.
> Her voice floats on a wide blue ocean of peace.
> Her words stitch the patches together.
> The story blankets the room with warmth.

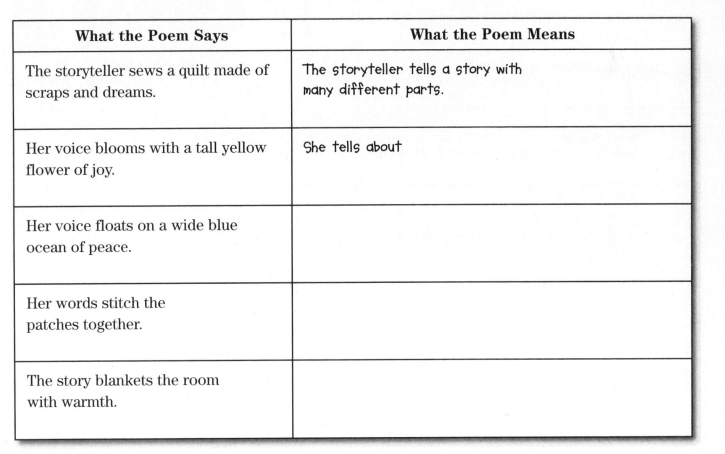

What the Poem Says	What the Poem Means
The storyteller sews a quilt made of scraps and dreams.	The storyteller tells a story with many different parts.
Her voice blooms with a tall yellow flower of joy.	She tells about
Her voice floats on a wide blue ocean of peace.	
Her words stitch the patches together.	
The story blankets the room with warmth.	

DIRECTIONS Draw a conclusion about the poem. How does the poet feel about storytellers or the stories they tell?

_____

_____

A Way With Words

DIRECTIONS Read the poem. Look for alliteration.
Underline the beginning sounds that repeat.

Alliteration

Alliteration is the repetition of beginning consonant sounds.

The ship sailed on the sea.
Tiny stars twinkled over the town.

Poets often use alliteration to give their poems a musical quality.

Sitting by the Sea

The sunlight spreads across the sand.

The waves whisper like the sound of the wind.

Feathers float on the foam by the water.

Birds bob and bounce on the waves.

Crabs creep into tiny rock caves.

The storyteller sees all these new sights.

Her words lead us through the waves and the water.

We delight in her dream of a day by the sea.

Birds bounce along the beach.

DIRECTIONS Write words with the same beginning sounds.
Use the words to write sentences with alliteration.

Words	Sentence
students, sing, song	The students sing a silly song.
boy, burgers, beach	